BUILDING THE PRIMARY CLASSROOM

A Handbook for Teacher Educators

Toni S. Bickart
Judy R. Jablon
Diane Trister Dodge

TEACHING STRATEGIES INC.

Washington, DC

Cover Photographs: Connie Reider and Andrew Edgar
Graphic Design and Production: Doug Gritzmacher

Published by:
Teaching Strategies, Inc.
P.O. Box 42243
Washington, DC 20015
www.TeachingStrategies.com

Printed and bound in the United States of America

First Printing: January 2001

ISBN: 1-879537-39-7
Library of Congress Catalog Number: 00-101015

Introduction

Instructional practices in the early elementary grades are under new scrutiny as expectations for children's learning rise. One effect of this emphasis on examining teaching practices is an increased focus on teacher training and staff development. This *Handbook*, designed as a companion to *Building the Primary Classroom*, will assist you in creating a staff development program within a school or school district and/or designing a course for teachers at the preservice or advanced degree level.

Building the Primary Classroom, with its focus on children in the early grades of elementary school, provides a practical framework for making teaching effective and learning meaningful. It offers teachers the tools and the rationale for planning a classroom environment based on a knowledge of young children and how they learn best. The *Handbook* suggests activities and shared reading and discussion techniques that implement and expand the concepts and messages of the book. Our goal is to develop teachers who know why they do what they do.

▶ What Effective Teachers Know

Without question, the goal of effective teaching is effective learning. Of course, children must gain knowledge and skills. They must also know how to apply what they have learned in new situations, how to solve problems, and how to ask questions that will lead to further learning. Thus, teachers must teach for understanding.

Teaching for understanding requires teachers to know about:

- Child development

- Pedagogy (knowledge of learning theory and teaching strategies)

- Curriculum content

Teachers with a solid background in child development know what children are like at different ages and use this information to plan for appropriate learning opportunities. In addition, because they know that children develop at different rates and have different strengths, teachers seek to know children as individuals, to learn about their cultural backgrounds and personal experiences, and to recognize how these experiences may affect their learning.

Using this knowledge about the children they teach and how children learn best, effective teachers employ a variety of teaching strategies to engage children in the learning process. They observe children purposefully, reflect on what is and isn't working, and make necessary changes.

Teachers in the elementary grades teach all subjects. Therefore, they need a knowledge base in all subject areas and an understanding of the continuum of learning in language and literacy, mathematics, social studies, science, technology, and the arts. This can be overwhelming unless teachers can find ways to integrate content into meaningful learning experiences that will engage children in learning what is required to meet state and local standards.

To create appropriate meaningful learning opportunities that truly engage children, teachers must integrate knowledge of child development, a variety of teaching strategies, and specific content knowledge. Though this is a tall order, this book can help.

Building the Primary Classroom shows how a conceptual framework of six strategies leads to effective teaching. Good teaching begins with **knowing children** in all their aspects. Through the process of **building a classroom community** teachers set the stage for using a broad range of teaching strategies. The **classroom structure** makes for an environment, schedule, and routines where significant learning can occur. Through the processes of **guiding** and **assessing children's learning**, teachers create the opportunities for specific learning in each discipline and integrated learning across content areas. **Building a partnership with families** gives teachers the added benefit of parent support and involvement.

A Framework for *Building the Primary Classroom*

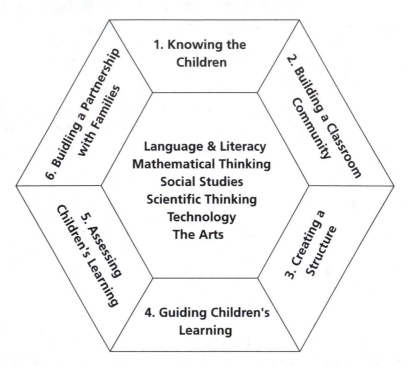

These strategies provide a foundation for content area instruction and are the focus of this *Handbook*. Although in many of the workshop activities we use material from the content area chapters to encourage reflective practice, we do not address curriculum content in depth in the *Handbook*. The Resources sections in each content chapter of *Building the Primary Classroom* include materials that discuss how to teach specific content.

▶ Using the *Handbook* with Different Audiences

The *Handbook* can facilitate your use of *Building the Primary Classroom* in a professional development program or college course. Its application depends upon the audience. We have found that the ideas in the book and the activities suggested engage people at many different levels. The *Handbook* is designed to be flexible—you can choose the topics to study, the activities to use, and the order in which to use them.

We believe that the *Handbook* models the approach to teaching and learning promoted in *Building the Primary Classroom*:

Learning is active. The activities in the *Handbook* are hands-on! Participants handle materials, think, talk, and collect ideas from others. Following each activity, the instructor/trainer and the group can analyze the effectiveness of the activity itself as well as the effectiveness of active learning.

Learning is challenging. We believe that adults (teachers), like children, construct their own understanding of new information. The methods used in the *Handbook* challenge teachers to reflect on current practice, question preconceived notions and beliefs, identify strategies that work, and learn new strategies to improve practice.

Learning is varied. We want teachers to see that one size does not fit all. Some information is delivered through lectures with overheads and handouts, some requires reading, both independent and shared. Other ideas are explored through hands-on experiential activities that are then analyzed. There are worksheets for individuals to complete and some that require the group to work together. Reflection may be done individually or as a group.

Learning is meaningful. The ideas addressed in the *Handbook* connect directly to the daily work of teaching and are thus relevant to each participant's work with children.

Learning is collaborative. The activities in the *Handbook* are structured so that participants practice different models of collaborative learning described in the book.

Professional Development Programs

Current thinking about professional development, supported by our own experiences working with teachers, aims to encourage all school personnel who interact with children to be responsible for increasing their own knowledge and skills. When this attitude permeates a school, there is likely to be more excitement, interest, and opportunity to talk about children's needs, teaching, and learning.

Those responsible for professional development—usually staff developers, principals, or curriculum coordinators—can influence the climate for growth. However, asking people to examine long-held beliefs and practices is difficult and requires that a process responding to individual and group needs be in place.

Listed below are some of the ways to create a positive climate for learning.

• Build a shared vision in which everyone who interacts with children feels valued and part of the continuous improvement effort.

• Make teacher collaboration an essential element of reform efforts. Studies repeatedly show that when teachers are encouraged to share ideas and plan curriculum content, they are much more likely to acquire new skills and change their instructional methods.

• Provide teachers with the time to plan and work together. Joint planning times are a prerequisite for teacher collaboration to work.

• Assure teachers that efforts to implement new approaches will be supported. Teachers need to know that they can try new ideas, make mistakes, and receive advice and encouragement from supervisors who will help them be successful.

The effect of these efforts is to create a climate of trust in a supportive environment. People are more willing to take risks and learn from their mistakes when they feel that they are all learning together.

Teacher Education Programs

Many college programs use *Building the Primary Classroom* as a text in teacher education courses that prepare students for initial certification and/or advanced degrees. This *Handbook* can be useful to professors preparing to teach a course with the text. Each strategy is introduced with an overview of the information contained in the text.

Some activities or workshops will require modification if students are not currently working in a classroom because they ask students to consider the children in their classroom as they do the activity. However, it is likely that students will be able to use previous experiences to connect what they have learned in theory courses to actual practice.

We hope you will try to structure your classes to reflect the principles and strategies used in the *Handbook* so your students experience the concepts under discussion firsthand. For example, consider holding class discussions with everyone sitting in a circle, arranging for small group work to be done at tables, and building time for reflection activities into every project.

Getting the Most from the *Handbook*

The Handbook follows the content and format of Part One of *Building the Primary Classroom*. It focuses on six teaching strategies:

- Knowing the Children You Teach

- Building a Classroom Community

- Establishing a Structure for the Classroom

- Guiding Children's Learning

- Assessing Children's Learning

- Building a Partnership with Families

Part Two of *Building the Primary Classroom* describes the six subject areas that teachers address in the primary grades. It shows how language and literacy, mathematical thinking, social studies, scientific thinking, technology, and the arts are taught within the *Building the Primary Classroom* framework. The workshops described in the *Handbook* show how the six strategies allow teachers to address curriculum content.

The Content and Format

The *Handbook* is divided into chapters for each of the six strategies. A chart at the beginning of each chapter lists the workshops related to that strategy (see example below). An overview section summarizes the basic content. If you wish, you can present a "mini lecture" using an overhead to highlight the major concepts. For each workshop topic, we indicate where the material is found in *Building the Primary Classroom*. Each workshop includes notes for the leader and the materials and estimated time required. The notes for each workshop include instructions in boldface. The bullets that follow these are suggested talking points.

To begin, we recommend that you read all the activities for each strategy. Then decide which activities best meet the needs, interests, and time constraints of your group. If the activities related to a given strategy are spaced out over time, participants can process the information and reflect on aspects of good practice.

WORKSHOP TOPICS	PURPOSE	MATERIALS	APPROXIMATE TIME
Overview	To provide an overview of the content of chapter one.	Notes, overhead p. 14	10-15 minutes
First impressions (relates to pp. 39-40)	To consider how relying on first impression affect our interactions and may lead to labeling children.	Notes, chart paper and markers p. 20	20-30 minutes
Developmental characteristics (relates to pp. 20-24)	To show how classroom practices are more likely to be successful if they are responsive to developmental characteristics of children.	Notes, handout p. 24	30-40 minutes
Individual characteristics (relates to pp. 25-33)	To identify ways children are unique and emphasize the value of building on children's strengths.	Notes, handout p. 28	40-50 minutes
The influence of culture (relates to pp. 34-38)	To consider how culture affects each person's communication patterns and expectations.	Notes, overhead p. 34	40-50 minutes

We use certain terms throughout the *Handbook*.

Jigsaw reading is a way of distributing the responsibility for reading among a group of people. Instead of everyone reading the same pages at the same time, each person in a group is given responsibility for reading a specific section or set of pages. Then each person shares the content by teaching the other members of his or her group.

Picture sets show particular classroom scenes. The object of the pictures is to stimulate ideas and encourage discussion of ways to incorporate the strategies from *Building the Primary Classroom* into a given situation. You can either create your own picture sets or use the illustrations in *Building the Primary Classroom*. For each workshop that requires a Picture Set, we suggest which illustrations to use and why.

Follow-up assignments are sometimes suggested after activities. These are designed to encourage practicing teachers to try discrete activities or new ways of doing things one step at a time. Student teachers may also be able to try some of these follow-ups. You may have to adapt activities for those students with no access to children in classrooms. When giving a follow-up assignment, allow time at the next class or workshop for teachers to come back to the group and share their experiences or reflections. In this way the group learns from the experiences of individual members, while individual members benefit from the group's comments and suggestions.

▶ Planning Your Course of Study

Whether you are planning a college course, a single workshop, or a yearlong series of staff development meetings, you will want to assess the needs of the group and establish appropriate goals. The six strategies provide a practical framework for planning, as well as a structure for thinking about curriculum. Listed below are some ideas to consider as you plan.

Ideas related to **Knowing Children**:

- Allocate time for "getting to know you" activities, particularly if students or participants do not know each other.

- Find out as much as possible about the students/participants in advance through interviews, observations, or pre-training assessments.

- Encourage alternative ways to express ideas (e.g., provide index cards or Post-its and encourage participants to write questions or comments throughout the classes).

- Ask participants to establish personal goals for the course of study.

Ideas related to **Building Community**:

- Use the steps in Abraham Maslow's "Hierarchy of Needs," (see page 47 of *Building the Primary Classroom*) to demonstrate how you will address the basic needs of the group. Consider room temperature, snack and restroom breaks, if appropriate, comfortable furniture, etc.

- Seat participants at tables that accommodate 4-6 people to promote collaboration. Proximity often fosters the sharing ideas and gives everyone an opportunity to participate.

- Create a meeting area for discussions where everyone can sit in a circle and see one another, if the group size is small enough (e.g., fewer than 30).

Ideas related to **Establishing Structure**:

- Try to make the physical environment of the room as attractive and welcoming as possible.

- Provide a list of topics to be considered and suggest any time constraints related to discussion or activities. You may want to post a chart at each session with a message about what will be happening that day.

- Involve participants in creating some rules or understandings about the way the class will operate and each person's responsibility for learning.

- Arrange in advance for the supplies and materials you need for each class (e.g., overhead projector, chart paper, easel, markers).

Ideas related to **Guiding Learning**:

- Include opportunities at each session for students/participants to construct their own understanding through personal or group investigations and by representing their thinking (e.g., writing, drawing, talking).

- Allocate time for participants to reflect on their learning (e.g., using journals, talking to one another).

- Allow sufficient time for the activities so that no one feels rushed.

- Include at each session open-ended activities that encompass multiple objectives. When teachers experience these types of activities as part of their own learning, they may be more comfortable using this approach in the classroom.

- Model the teacher as facilitator. Call attention to the amount of learning that occurs when you are not talking. Encourage reflection and the sharing of ideas by suggesting that each person consider multiple answers to a question. Model different ways to do this such as: encouraging individual reflection; suggesting that participants turn to a neighbor to discuss a question, then share their thoughts with the group; or asking small groups to discuss something and then explain their ideas to the large group.

Ideas related to **Assessing Learning**:

- Develop an evaluation form if you want written feedback on each class or session.

- Plan a variety of ways to get feedback (e.g., journal entries that you read and react to).

- If you are working with practicing teachers, take time between classes for teachers to observe one another—if they wish—and to try out different approaches. If you are working with preservice teachers, encourage them to observe teachers and research the methods they use to assess children.

- Encourage participants to use a journal during the class to keep track of questions, react to what they are learning, and record their classroom experiences as they implement or observe some of the ideas and approaches. Ask participants to submit reflections on a regular basis and provide individual feedback.

Using some of these ideas enables you to incorporate the strategies into the structure of your course or professional development program.

How to Begin

It is easy to begin teaching with the *Handbook*. First, be sure that each student in the class or participant in the program has a copy of *Building the Primary Classroom*. Emphasize that this will be the basic text and reference for the course. You may want to invite students to browse through the book to observe its structure and general contents.

Begin instruction with the opening activity, "The Successful Learner," that follows this Introduction. "The Successful Learner" is designed to foster thinking about the big goals of education. A discussion of these goals leads into an overview of the framework of six strategies. From that point you've established the tenor of the program and can choose the activities you think will provide the greatest motivation for your group.

References

Bransford, John D., Ann L. Brown, and Rodney R. Cocking, editors, National Research Council. *How People Learn: Brain, Mind, Experience, and School*. Washington, DC: National Academy Press, 1999.

Donovan, M. Suzanne, John D. Bransford, and James W. Pellegrino, editors, National Research Council. *How People Learn: Bridging Research and Practice*. Washington, DC: National Academy Press, 1999.

Tomlinson, Carol Ann. *The Differentiated Classroom: Responding to the Needs of All Learners*. Alexandria, VA: Association for Supervision and Curriculum Development, 1999.

The Successful Learner

▶ **Introduce the topic**

- All of us want children to be successful learners.

▶ **Invite participants to think about the meaning of "successful learners"**

- Take a minute to think of children you have taught or adults you know, who you feel are successful learners. Think about two or three characteristics that you feel make that person a successful learner.

▶ **Invite participants to discuss their ideas with a neighbor**

- Turn to the person next to you and share your ideas.

▶ **When participants are ready, invite ideas from the whole group**

- Please share with us your ideas.
    Participants' ideas may include the following:
    ◊ *curiosity*
    ◊ *independence*
    ◊ *willingness to take risks*
    ◊ *initiative*
    ◊ *responsibility*
    ◊ *creativity*
    ◊ *asking questions*
    ◊ *perseverance*

▶ **Put on overhead and distribute handout "Characteristics of a Successful Learner"**

- These are what Lilian Katz calls the dispositions to be a learner.

- This is what teaching and learning should be about—nurturing these characteristics.

▶ Summarize the key concepts

- If this is what we want children to learn, then anything we do to discourage the development of these skills and attitudes works against our central goals.

- **How** we teach children is certainly as important as **what** we teach. Or, rather, the way we teach children will greatly influence whether and how much children learn.

- There is growing consensus among educators today that instructional methods which emphasize drills, worksheets, and the teaching of skills in isolation do not help children become competent learners.

- Competent learners can define a problem, find information, put ideas together, and apply knowledge to new situations.

- *Building the Primary Classroom* begins with what we know about how children learn and shows how teachers can apply that knowledge in the classroom.

- *Building the Primary Classroom* also recognizes the importance of helping children develop social competence—the ability to work with others, share ideas, and communicate effectively.

- Teachers today are faced with so many agendas—there is the content they are expected to teach and multiple instructional methods and approaches they are urged to incorporate (e.g. cooperative learning, conflict resolution, literature-based instruction, hands-on math). They have to decide how it all fits together.

▶ Put on overhead

- This is the framework for *Building the Primary Classroom*. The six strategies are based on current research and the experiences of successful teachers.

- Implementing these strategies in the classroom enables teachers to have a framework for making teaching effective and learning meaningful for children.

Introduce "Knowing the Children"

- Knowing the children you teach means understanding developmental stages, individual characteristics, and the influence of culture. Because every group is unique, teaching is a dynamic process, shaped in part by the attributes and interests of each group of children.

Introduce "Building a Classroom Community"

- Building a classroom community involves having daily class meetings, helping children learn to work collaboratively, and teaching children social problem-solving skills. When a classroom functions as a community, children experience a sense of belonging and a sense of empowerment that are essential to their well-being and their academic success.

Introduce "Establishing a Structure for the Classroom"

- Everyone—children and adults—need structure. Establishing a structure for the classroom involves organizing the classroom environment, establishing consistent schedules and routines, and conveying specific expectations for behavior. An explicit structure enables teachers to facilitate children's learning and helps children to become self-directed learners.

Introduce "Guiding Children's Learning"

- Guiding children's learning describes how teachers create opportunities for children to acquire skills and content as children actively investigate, represent, and reflect on their increasing understanding of the world around them. Teachers organize the curriculum using an integrated approach that allows children to apply skills they are learning in math, reading, writing, science, social studies, technology, and the arts.

Introduce "Assessing Children's Learning"

- Assessing children's learning occurs every day as teachers observe children and collect samples of their work. A comprehensive approach to assessment enables teachers to make informed decisions about curriculum, plan instruction, monitor, and share children's progress with families in a meaningful way.

▶ Introduce "Building a Partnership with Families"

- Building a partnership with families means taking time to learn about each child's family, involving families in the school community, establishing a structure for ongoing communication, sharing the curriculum, and involving families in the assessment process. When families are involved, children's achievement is enhanced, teachers obtain critically important support, and schools become better places for learning.

▶ Distribute handout "Principles about Teaching and Learning"

- Out of these strategies have come 14 principles about teaching and learning.

- Take a few minutes to review these principles. Mark 3 or 4 that you feel are most important for you personally.

▶ When participants are ready, summarize the topic

- These principles underlie the instructional approach described in *Building the Primary Classroom*. They are equally applicable to effective adult learning experiences.

Characteristics of a Successful Learner*

- curiosity

- independence

- responsibility

- initiative

- creativity

- willingness to take risks

- ask questions

- perseverance

*Katz, Lilian and Sylvia Chard. *Engaging Children's Minds: The Project Approach.* Norwood, NJ: Ablex Publishing Co., 1989, p. 30.

A Framework for
Building the Primary Classroom

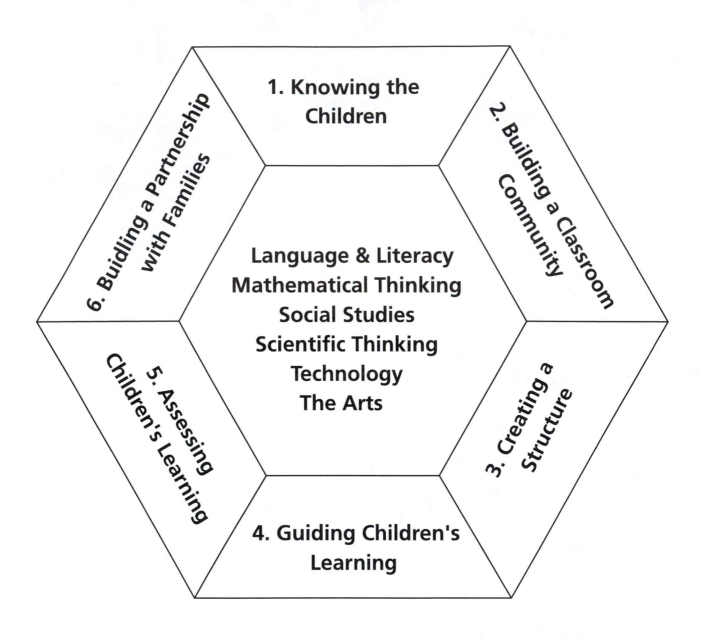

1. Knowing the Children

2. Building a Classroom Community

3. Creating a Structure

4. Guiding Children's Learning

5. Assessing Children's Learning

6. Buidling a Partnership with Families

Language & Literacy
Mathematical Thinking
Social Studies
Scientific Thinking
Technology
The Arts

Principles About Teaching and Learning

1. Each person has preferred ways of taking in new information.

2. People bring their own experiences and ways of perceiving to new situations.

3. Learning takes place in an environment in which people feel safe and respected.

4. Social interaction fosters learning.

5. A clear structure helps people feel comfortable because they know what to expect.

6. Learners feel empowered when they have opportunities to choose what and how they will learn.

7. People are motivated to learn when they have a reason and desire to find something out.

8. Learners construct knowledge by relating new information to what they already know.

9. Meaningful learning requires time to think and opportunities to revisit ideas.

10. Learning requires active investigation: questioning, exploring, and researching.

11. The personal expression of ideas (representation) solidifies understanding.

12. Reflection promotes self-awareness about what is being learned and how.

13. Teaching and learning are a shared endeavor and a joint responsibility.

14. Instruction is most effective when it reflects the needs and interests of the learner.

1

KNOWING
THE CHILDREN
YOU TEACH

Chapter 1 Workshops

WORKSHOP TOPICS	PURPOSE	MATERIALS	APPROXIMATE TIME
Overview	To provide an overview of the content of chapter one.	Notes, overhead, handout p. 20	10-15 minutes
First impressions (relates to pp. 39-40)	To consider how relying on first impression affect our interactions and may lead to labeling children.	Notes, chart paper and markers p. 26	20-30 minutes
Developmental characteristics (relates to pp. 20-24)	To show how classroom practices are more likely to be successful if they are responsive to developmental characteristics of children.	Notes, handout p. 30	30-40 minutes
Individual characteristics (relates to pp. 25-33)	To identify ways children are unique and emphasize the value of building on children's strengths.	Notes, handout p. 34	40-50 minutes
The influence of culture (relates to pp. 34-38)	To consider how culture affects each person's communication patterns and expectations.	Notes, overhead, handout p. 40	40-50 minutes

Overview

▶ Introduce the topic

- The foundation for building the primary classroom is knowing about children developmentally and individually. That is why it is the first strategy.

- Knowing the children you teach influences the kinds of learning experiences you plan.

- Knowing children well makes it possible to build positive relationships with them, which is often the key to their success in school.

▶ Put on overhead

- This overhead highlights the three ways of knowing the children you teach: developmentally, individually, and in the context of culture.

- I will give a brief overview of what is addressed in each section. You have this as a handout if you wish to take notes.

▶ Discuss developmental stages

- Understanding child development helps teachers to know how and why children behave as they do and what to expect of children at a given statge of development.

- Curriculum is considered "age appropriate" or "developmentally appropriate" if it is based on a knowledge of children's social, emotional, cognitive, and physical characteristics.

- Social development addresses how a child relates to others, including the ability to make friends.

- Emotional development relates to feelings about self and others.

- Cognitive development refers to how a child thinks, processes information, solves problems, and uses language.

- Physical development includes growth in size, strength, motor skills, and coordination.

- It is important to remember that although we can look at each area of development separately, all areas are interrelated. In addition, we know that all children do not grow and develop at the same rate.

▶ Discuss individual characteristics

- The individual characteristics of children include their temperament, interests and talents, learning differences, life experiences, and resiliency.

- Temperament refers to a person's mental outlook—whether they are shy or outgoing, active or quiet.

- Children bring different interests and talents to the classroom. When teachers know children's individual interests and talents, they can support their growth and learning more effectively.

- Learning differences refer to how each child prefers to take in new information—their particular learning style. This affects how a child best absorbs information. In addition, children have special skills or strengths that reflect different types of intelligence as we have learned from the work of Howard Gardner.

- Children's life experiences also contribute to who they are as individuals—their family of origin, previous experiences in school, community, and so on.

- You may have children in your classroom who come from families with severe problems, such as drug abuse or health problems. While some may label these children "at risk," it is more helpful to look for the strength or resilience these children demonstrate. When you focus on strengths you can give children opportunities to practice helpful behaviors.

- And some children have special needs. These can include a child with a diagnosed disability, a child in crisis, or a child who is gifted. Teachers must be knowledgeable about the laws related to inclusion and what support children with special needs are entitled to receive.

▶ Discuss cultural influences

- The cultural context in which children have been raised influences their communication and interaction styles and expectations about behavior.

- When children come from a culture different from that of the teacher, the teacher may have difficulty interpreting their ways of communicating. Some children may not understand the teacher's ways.

- We need to guard against misinterpretations and strive toward understanding.

- Therefore, an essential step in knowing children is taking the time to learn about a child's cultural background.

Knowing the Children You Teach

- Developmental Stages

- Individual Characteristics

- Cultural Influences

Chapter 1 Workshops

WORKSHOP TOPICS	PURPOSE	MATERIALS	APPROXIMATE TIME
Overview	To provide an overview of the content of chapter one	Notes, overhead, handout p. 20	10-15 minutes
First impressions (relates to pp. 39-40)	To consider how relying on first impression affect our interactions and may lead to labeling children	Notes, chart paper and markers p. 26	20-30 minutes
Developmental characteristics (relates to pp. 20-24)	To show how classroom practices are more likely to be successful if they are responsive to developmental characteristics of children	Notes, handout p. 30	30-40 minutes
Individual characteristics (relates to pp. 25-33)	To identify ways children are unique and emphasize the value of building on children's strengths.	Notes, handout p. 34	40-50 minutes
The influence of culture (relates to pp. 34-38)	To consider how culture affects each person's communication patterns and expectations.	Notes, overhead, handout p. 40	40-50 minutes

First Impressions

Note to teacher educators:

Please note that this activity is ONLY effective with groups where the participants can be paired with someone they do not know.

There are two possible places to use this activity. You may do it after you have given an overview of Knowing Children. Or, you may choose to use it as a warm-up before introducing the section, Knowing Children. If you do it as a warm-up, you can discuss or debrief at this point.

▶ Introduce the activity

- We are going to do an activity. Please find someone you don't know and sit next to that person.

▶ Give instructions

- When you are seated, imagine that you have just gotten on a train and your partner, a total stranger, is seated next to you. You don't speak to one another; you look one another over, and speculate about each other.

- Of course this is an odd thing for me to ask you to do. While I'm sure we all do this all the time, it isn't something to practice! But, for this activity let your imagination soar.

- On a piece of paper, jot down some hypotheses that you have about the person based entirely on how they look. You might try to guess your partner's
    ◊ level of education
    ◊ personality
    ◊ job
    ◊ family background
    ◊ interests/hobbies

- You will **not** have to share your impressions.

▶ When participants are ready, give the next instructions

- Now take about five minutes to interview one another. You might ask:
  ◊ What would you like to tell me about yourself?
  ◊ Where did you grow up?
  ◊ What are your professional interests and goals?
  ◊ What are some of your personal interests?

▶ Invite partners to process with each other

- When you have finished interviewing each other, take a few minutes to discuss your reactions to the exercise.
  ◊ How do your first impressions match up or differ from what you learned in the interview?
  ◊ What factors influence our first impressions of children (e.g. personal appearance and behavior)?
  ◊ What insights did this activity spark regarding your work with children?

▶ Reconvene the large group

- Please share with us your reactions to this experience.

- What ideas will you take with you?
  ◊ How can we avoid labeling children based on first impressions?
  ◊ What steps can you take to get to know children well and go beyond first impressions?

▶ Refer participants to *Building the Primary Classroom*

- On pages 34-35 in *Building the Primary Classroom,* there are suggestions for getting to know children.

- Take a few minutes to review them.

Chapter 1 Workshops

WORKSHOP TOPICS	PURPOSE	MATERIALS	APPROXIMATE TIME
Overview	To provide an overview of the content of chapter one.	Notes, overhead, handout p. 20	10-15 minutes
First impressions (relates to pp. 39-40)	To consider how relying on first impression affect our interactions and may lead to labeling children.	Notes, chart paper and markers p. 26	20-30 minutes
Developmental characteristics (relates to pp. 20-24)	To show how classroom practices are more likely to be successful if they are responsive to developmental characteristics of children.	Notes, handout p. 30	30-40 minutes
Individual characteristics (relates to pp. 25-33)	To identify ways children are unique and emphasize the value of building on children's strengths.	Notes, handout p. 34	40-50 minutes
The influence of culture (relates to pp. 34-38)	To consider how culture affects each person's communication patterns and expectations.	Notes, overhead, handout p. 40	40-50 minutes

Developmental Characteristics

▶ Introduce the topic

- "Developmentally appropriate" practice means that classroom practices are responsive to the characteristics of children at a given stage of development.

- Development is one aspect of who children are that is fairly predictable.

▶ Introduce activity

- This activity is designed to show that teachers have choices in designing classroom practices. Their practices can either be responsive to children's developmental characteristics, or unresponsive.

▶ Distribute Handout, "Responding to Developmental Characteristics"

- The middle column of this handout lists typical developmental characteristics of primary grade children. It asks you to think of practices that are responsive to each developmental characteristic, and practices that fail to respond to these characteristics.

▶ Provide an example

- Let's try an example. One common characteristic of primary grade children, especially first graders, is that they all want to be first. You may have noticed that first graders typically argue over who is first in line or who gets to try an activity first.

▶ Elicit ideas of practices that fail to respond to developmental characteristics

- What practices might fail to respond to children's need to be first?
  Participants may give examples such as:
  ◊ *Telling children to line up but failing to establish a system so everyone runs to be first.*
  ◊ *Reprimanding children and having them practice lining up properly.*
  ◊ *Planning competitive games in which only one or two children get to win or be first.*

- What are some consequences of failing to respond to this need to be first?
  Participants may give examples such as:
  ◊ *Children fighting with each other.*
  ◊ *Children being punished and feeling bad.*

▶ **Elicit ideas of practices that are responsive to developmental characteristics**

- Knowing that wanting to be first is a typical characteristic of young children, what are some practices that would be more responsive to children's needs and interests?
  Participants may give examples such as:
  ◊ *Having jobs such as "line leaders" and "meeting starter," and rotating them regularly.*
  ◊ *Encouraging children who have particular skills to teach them to others.*

▶ **Give instructions. Assist groups as needed**

- Take 10-15 minutes at your tables to discuss the developmental characteristics of primary grade children listed on your handout and brainstorm practices that would be responsive to developmental characteristics, and ones that would fail to respond.

▶ **Call the group back and invite them to share any insights and ideas**

- Let's take a few minutes to have each group share some of the practices you identified and discussed.

▶ **Refer participants to *Building the Primary Classroom***

- In your book on pages 20-24, you will find a chart that shows how teachers can respond to a range of developmental characteristics of primary grade children. Take a few minutes to review this chart, especially the practices related to characteristics you discussed.

▶ **Allow time for reading**

- Would some of you like to share your reactions?

▶ **Summarize the topic**

- Awareness of child development helps teachers plan an environment and activities that will promote success for children. These practices are discussed throughout the book.

Responding to Developmental Characteristics

Understanding child development helps teachers know how and why children behave as they do and what to expect of children within each age group. Our teaching practices are considered "developmentally appropriate" if they are based on knowledge of what most children can do and how they think and learn at a particular stage of development.

Practices that **fail** to respond to these developmental characteristics	Developmental Characteristics of Primary Grade Children	Practices that are **responsive** to these developmental characteristics
	Emotional Characteristics	
	Sensitive to teasing, insults, and put-downs	
	Act self-assured but still have many self-doubts	
	Social Characteristics	
	Eager to make friends and be with peers but not always successful at doing so	
	Eager to be independent of adults and may challenge authority	
	Cognitive Characteristics	
	Increasingly skilled and interested in reading and expressing thoughts verbally and in writing	
	Ask questions that are fact oriented—How, Why, When	
	Physical Characteristics	
	Active and energetic but may tire suddenly	
	Likely to become hungry in mid-morning and have low energy	

Chapter 1 Workshop

WORKSHOP TOPICS	PURPOSE	MATERIALS	APPROXIMATE TIME
Overview	To provide an overview of the content of chapter one.	Notes, overhead, handout p. 20	10-15 minutes
First impressions (relates to pp. 39-40)	To consider how relying on first impression affect our interactions and may lead to labeling children.	Notes, chart paper and markers p. 26	20-30 minutes
Developmental characteristics (relates to pp. 20-24)	To show how classroom practices are more likely to be successful if they are responsive to developmental characteristics of children.	Notes, handout p. 30	30-40 minutes
Individual characteristics (relates to pp. 25-33)	To identify ways children are unique and emphasize the value of building on children's strengths.	Notes, handout p. 34	40-50 minutes
The influence of culture (relates to pp. 34-38)	To consider how culture affects each person's communication patterns and expectations.	Notes, overhead, handout p. 40	40-50 minutes

Individual Characteristics

Note to teacher educators:

In this activity, participants write the names of the children in their classrooms. Classroom teachers or preservice teachers in student-teacher positions will be able to do this. If you are teaching those who are not in classrooms with children, you will have to modify this workshop to make it work. You might ask your students to list the names of 10 friends and indentify a strength, talent, or special interest for each. Then ask how this knowledge affects the relationship with the friend.

▶ **Introduce the key concepts**

- A second way of knowing children is recognizing that each child is a unique individual.

- For children to thrive as learners, the classroom must be a place where everyone feels comfortable and valued for their unique qualities.

▶ **Distribute Handout, "Learning about the Individual Characteristics of Children"**

- The first part of this activity is an individual task.

- Draw a line under the number of children in your classroom. If you have more than 26 children, continue the numbers on the back of the sheet.

- Now write the names of all the children in your class.

▶ **Invite participants to reflect or share what they learned**

- Take a few minutes to reflect on the following questions:
    ◊ Were you able to think of all the children in your class?
    ◊ Which children did you list first?
    ◊ Why were they easy to remember?
    ◊ Did you forget anyone?

- Discuss your response to this activity with the people at your table.

▶ Give the next instructions

- The second part of this activity is to identify a strength, talent, or special interest for each child in your class.

- Write down something you know about each child in the right-hand column. Think of positive characteristics and strengths.

▶ Note when participants seem to have written as much as they can

- Are you surprised by how much you know about the children in your class?

- Were there any children you weren't able to say something about?

- How might you find out about something special about these children?

- How can you (or do you) use what you know about each child to develop a positive relationship and help the child experience success.

▶ Introduce jigsaw reading

- In *Building the Primary Classroom,* on pages 25-33, you will find six ways in which children are unique.

- Have the people at your table each take one section to read and then share what you learned from your section with the rest of your group.

▶ Summarize and give follow-up assignment

- Every classroom contains a diverse group of individuals; there is no such thing as a homogeneous group of children.

- There are also many different aspects that make up a child's individuality.

- Take this handout with you and continue to learn about what takes each child special.

- Think about ways you can use what you learn to build a positive relationship with each child.

Learning About the Individual Characteristics of Children

Each child brings a unique combination of characteristics and experiences to the classroom. These distinctive qualities affect how each child learns and relates to others. When classrooms are places where every individual feels comfortable and valued, children have a greater chance of being successful learners.

1. Use the space on the left to make a list of all the children in your class. Continue on the back of this sheet if your group is larger.

2. Think about each child. Identify a strength/talent/special interest each child beings to the classroom.

Child's Name	A strength/talent/special interest the child brings to the classroom
1.	
2.	
3.	
4.	
5.	
6.	
7.	
8.	
9.	
10.	
11.	
12.	
13.	
14.	
15.	
16.	
17.	
18.	
19.	
20.	
21.	
22.	
23.	
24.	
25.	

Chapter 1 Workshop

WORKSHOP TOPICS	PURPOSE	MATERIALS	APPROXIMATE TIME
Overview	To provide an overview of the content of chapter one.	Notes, overhead, handout p. 20	10-15 minutes
First impressions (relates to pp. 39-40)	To consider how relying on first impression affect our interactions and may lead to labeling children.	Notes, chart paper and markers p. 26	20-30 minutes
Developmental characteristics (relates to pp. 20-24)	To show how classroom practices are more likely to be successful if they are responsive to developmental characteristics of children.	Notes, handout p. 30	30-40 minutes
Individual characteristics (relates to pp. 25-33)	To identify ways children are unique and emphasize the value of building on children's strengths.	Notes, handout p. 34	40-50 minutes
The influence of culture (relates to pp. 34-38)	To consider how culture affects each person's communication patterns and expectations.	Notes, overhead, handout p. 40	40-50 minutes

The Influence of Culture

▶ **Introduce the topic**

- A third way to know the children you teach is to learn about the child's culture.

▶ **Invite participants to think about the meaning of "culture"**

- Let's take a few minutes to personally think about what culture means.

▶ **Allow about 10 minutes, then list each table's ideas on a chart**

- Please talk with the people at your table and come up with a group definition. We'll then share each table's definition.
  Participants may suggest the following:
  ◊ *A group you identify with.*
  ◊ *A system of values and beliefs that bring people together.*
  ◊ *The way a group of people behave together.*
  ◊ *The standards by which we judge ourselves and others.*

▶ **Summarize the key concepts**

- Culture affects how we communicate and interact with others and the kinds of expectations we have.

- Each of us has a set of beliefs about ourselves as well as values, attitudes, assumptions, and expectations about people and events around us.

- It is easier for us to relate to and understand people from similar cultural backgrounds.

- Therefore, the greater the difference between a teacher's cultural background and that of the children, the more effort the teacher must make to learn about the culture of the children.

▶ Put on overhead and distribute handout if you wish

- In *Building the Primary Classroom*, the section on culture discusses two ways that culture affects each of us.

- The first is how we communicate with others—our words, actions, postures, gestures, tone of voice, facial expression, the way we handle time, space and materials.

- The second way in which culture influences us is expectations—what we view as acceptable behavior.

▶ Give instruction for jigsaw reading

- *Building the Primary Classroom* discusses culture and communication on pages 34-37, and culture and expectations on pages 37-38.

- Each person at your table should select one of the sections to read. Take a few minutes to reflect on what you read. You can use the handout to record your reactions.

- Share your reactions to the section you read with others at your table.

▶ Ask participants to apply the reading to personal experience

- Have you ever had the experience of being misperceived?

- Have you ever misinterpreted something another person or a child said or did?

- Would anyone be willing to share a personal experience?

▶ Summarize the topic

- Most classrooms today reflect the rich diversity of American society.

- It would be impossible to expect a teacher to know a great deal about every cultural group rep resented.

- Parents and other family members can be excellent resources for teachers who are open to learning about a child's background.

- Being open to the many ways in which children (and all of us) are influenced by our cultural background is an important step in getting to know each child.

Understanding the Influence of Culture

- Culture and Communication

- Culture and Expectations

2

BUILDING
A CLASSROOM
COMMUNITY

Chapter 2 Workshops

WORKSHOP TOPICS	PURPOSE	MATERIALS	APPROXIMATE TIME
Overview	To provide an overview of the content of chapter two.	Notes, overhead, handout p. 48	10-15 minutes
Defining Community (relates to pp. 46-51)	To consider different kinds of communities and how communities have changed.	Notes, overhead, handouts, markers, chart paper, tape p. 54	20-30 minutes
Welcoming Children to the Classroom (relates to pp. 52-56)	To identify what teachers can do before school and in the first few days to introduce children to the classroom community.	Notes, community picture set, chart paper, markers, tape p. 60	20-30 minutes
How Meetings Build Community (relates to pp. 57-65]	To consider different formats for addressing the whole group and exploring what makes meetings work.	Notes, handout, chart paper, markers p. 64	30-40 minutes
Fostering Meaningful Discussions	To analyze factors that make discussions purposeful and develop plans for conducting meetings.	Notes, two copies of Planning Handout and Meeting Handout p. 70	40-50 minutes

Overview

▶ **Introduce the second strategy**

- The second strategy in *Building the Primary Classroom* is Building a Classroom Community.

- Every classroom, like every community, has its own distinct culture, values, and rules.

- Children, as well as teachers, belong to many different communities.

- The classroom community is the one you build with children to help them feel connected to other people at school.

- Building a sense of community in the classroom enables you to address children's social, emotional, and cognitive development.

▶ **Put on overhead and distribute handout, "Building a Classroom Community"**

- This overhead highlights the six sections of the chapter on Building a Classroom Community.

- I will give a brief overview of what is addressed in each section. You have this as a handout if you wish to take notes.

▶ **Discuss the value of a classroom community**

- Children learn best when their basic needs are met. Abraham Maslow's "Hierarchy of Needs" provides a useful framework for considering what children need in order to learn.

- A classroom community provides a setting in which children can practice behaviors associated with resiliency. This is especially important for children who have had experiences that threaten their sense of security and safety.

- Problem-solving experiences in a community build initiative in children. When children work with others successfully they form relationships. The ability to demonstrate initiative and form relationships are characteristics of children who are resilient.

- Teaching children respect and responsibility is also part of the curriculum and can best be achieved when the classroom functions as a community where children are treated respectfully. They gain experience in making decisions and having responsibilities.

- Because friends are so important to primary grade children, a classroom community must support children in getting along with their peers.

- A final value of a classroom community is that it is one of the most effective ways to promote inclusion of children with disabilities.

Discuss welcoming children to the classroom community

- Teachers begin building a classroom community before school starts. This section shows how teachers plan for children and orient them to their new environment.

Discuss using meetings to build a sense of community

- Effective communication is central to building a community. Meetings offer a way for all community members to talk as a group and share ideas.

- For meetings to be effective, teachers must support children in learning how to talk and listen and engage in meaningful discussions.

- Many different types of meetings occur during the course of a day—for example, meetings to start the day, to introduce new materials or a lesson, to have a discussion or share information.

▶ Discuss helping children relate positively to others

- A community functions well if individuals know how to relate positively to others. Teachers cannot assume that all children come with these skills.

- Therefore, building a classroom community involves modeling respectful interactions, helping all children feel competent, teaching friendship-making skills, and teaching children how to work collaboratively.

▶ Discuss promoting social problem-solving skills

- Conflicts inevitably arise—they are part of life. All children need to know how to solve problems and resolve conflicts peacefully.

- Teaching the skills of social problem solving is part of building community and an important critical thinking skill.

- When children are engaged in social problem solving with individuals and as a class, they learn to appreciate differences and learn a process for resolving conflicts and making decisions that work for all.

▶ Discuss the school as community

- Schools can function as a community—a place where each person feels respected and involved.

- Taking on school-wide projects, creating opportunities for teachers to share new approaches, and involving families in school life are ways that a sense of community can be promoted.

Building A Classroom Community

- The Value of a Classroom Community

- Welcoming Children to the Classroom Community

- Using Meetings to Build a Sense of Community

- Helping Children Relate Positively to Others

- Promoting Social Problem-Solving Skills

- The School as a Community

Chapter 2 Workshops

WORKSHOP TOPICS	PURPOSE	MATERIALS	APPROXIMATE TIME
Overview	To provide an overview of the content of chapter one.	Notes, overhead, handout p. 48	10-15 minutes
Defining Community (relates to pp. 46-51)	To consider different kinds of communities and how communities have changed.	Notes, overhead handouts, markers chart paper, tape p. 54	20-30 minutes
Welcoming Children to the Classroom (relates to pp. 52-56)	To identify what teachers can do before school and in the first few days to introduce children to the classroom community.	Notes, community picture set, chart paper, markers, tape p. 60	20-30 minutes
How Meetings Build Community (relates to pp. 57-65)	To consider different formats for addressing the whole group and exploring what makes meetings work.	Notes, handout, chart paper, markers p. 64	30-40 minutes
Fostering Meaningful Discussions	To analyze factors that make discussions purposeful and develop plans for conducting meetings.	Notes, two copies of Planning Handout and Meeting Handout p. 70	40-50 minutes

Defining Community

▸ **Introduce the term "community" then list the types of communities on a chart**

- All of us belong to many different communities. Think of some of the communities you belong to.
    Participants may give suggestions such as:
    ◊ *neighborhood*
    ◊ *clubs*
    ◊ *religious group*
    ◊ *music group*
    ◊ *sports club*

- Take a few moments to think about your involvement in these communities. What does it mean to you to be a part of a community?

- Talk to a partner about what it means to you. Then we'll share ideas as a group.

▸ **As they offer them, list ideas on what it means to be part of a community**

  Participants' ideas may include the following:
  ◊ *you feel you belong*
  ◊ *you share common goals*
  ◊ *you have something to contribute to others and you get something from others*
  ◊ *you feel valued*
  ◊ *you are interested in what happens and involved*

▸ **Summarize the discussion**

- A community is built around the shared interests, values, and goals of its members.

- Building a classroom community gives children a common and predictable culture that helps them feel connected to others.

▶ **Distribute Handout, "Changing Communities." Allow 5 minutes for question #1**

- The first part of this activity is an individual task.

- Take a few minutes to reflect on question #1 in this handout. Jot down any ideas that come to mind.

▶ **Allow about 10 minutes for the group discussion**

- Turn to the people near you and take a few minutes to share your memories and reflections. You can use the space under question 2 to record common themes that may emerge.

- Compare and contrast what communities are like today for children and families.

- Think about the implications for the classroom today.

▶ **Pull the group together and invite the small groups to share their discussions**

- Did you identify any common themes as you shared your personal reflections?

- In what ways can teachers and schools provide a sense of community for children and families today?

▶ **Put on overhead and distribute "The Value of Building a Classroom Community"**

- Teachers have many challenges today as they work to meet the needs of children and ensure their success in school.

- Taking time to build a classroom community can help teachers address children's needs in five ways. A classroom community helps teachers:
    - ◊ address children's basic needs;
    - ◊ promote resiliency;
    - ◊ teach respect and responsibility;
    - ◊ promote social and academic competence; and
    - ◊ support inclusion of all children.

▶ Give instructions for jigsaw reading

- In *Building the Primary Classroom*, pages 46-51 discuss the five advantages to building a classroom community.

- Have the people at your table each take one section to read and then share what you learned.

- You can use the handout to record your thoughts and any ideas you want to remember.

▶ Distribute chart paper and markers

- To summarize your discussion, think about the underlying message you wish to communicate to children in your classroom. Complete the following sentence on the chart paper: "In our classroom, we work on building a community because . . ."

- When you have written your message, please post it on the wall.

- To summarize this session, I'd like one person from each group to read the group's message.

Changing Communities

1. Take a few moments to think back on the community in which you grew up.
    Write down your thoughts as you reflect on the following questions:

    *   Describe the kinds of activities that brought the community together.

    *   In what ways did families get involved in the community?

    *   What role did the school play in the community?

    *   What was it like being a child in your community?

2. In small groups of 2 to 4 people, share your memories and recollections.
    Find common themes. Write them down.

3. Compare and contrast what communities are like today for children and families.
    What are the implications for teachers of young children?

The Value of Building a Classroom Community

- Addressing Children's Basic Needs

- Promoting Resiliency

- Teaching Respect and Responsibility

- Promoting Children's Social and Academic Competence

- Supporting Inclusion of All Children

Chapter 2 Workshops

WORKSHOP TOPICS	PURPOSE	MATERIALS	APPROXIMATE TIME
Overview	To provide an overview of the content of chapter one.	Notes, overhead, handout p. 48	10-15 minutes
Defining Community (relates to pp. 46-51)	To consider different kinds of communities and how communities have changed.	Notes, overhead handouts, markers chart paper, tape p. 54	20-30 minutes
Welcoming Children to the Classroom (relates to pp. 52-56)	To identify what teachers can do before school and in the first few days to introduce children to the classroom community.	Notes, tape community picture set, chart paper, markers p. 60	20-30 minutes
How Meetings Build Community (relates to pp. 57-65)	To consider different formats for addressing the whole group and exploring what makes meetings work.	Notes, handout, chart paper, markers p. 64	30-40 minutes
Fostering Meaningful Discussions	To analyze factors that make discussions purposeful and develop plans for conducting meetings.	Notes, two copies of Planning Handout and Meeting Handout p. 70	40-50 minutes

Welcoming Children to the Classroom

Note to teacher educators:

This workshop involves participants in examining a variety of pictures of classrooms to encourage discussion about multiple ways to build a sense of community. Community is built through the kinds of displays on the walls, the way materials are used, how children interact, the projects children do, and how topics are studied.

You can either create your own set of pictures to use or have participants discuss some of the illustrations in *Building the Primary Classroom.*We recommend the following illustrations for discussion:

- Page 53: Interesting People, Interesting Information
- Page 57: A class meeting
- Page 109: Shared writing materials
- Page 152: Group planning, problem solving
- Page 167: Children working together
- Page 169: Shared art materials
- Page 288: Shared books
- Page 328: Group art project
- Page 336: Group working together in math
- Page 351 and 361: We study things together
- Page 409: Group design, construction project

If you would like to add some photographs to use with these illustrations, you might try to include pictures of scenes such as the following:

- Self-portraits of children hanging in a classroom
- An attendance system on display that shows who is here and who is absent
- A room with children's work on the walls
- A display of photographs of the children
- A display that relates information about the children in the classroom, e.g., birthdays or favorite ice cream flavors

▶ Elicit ideas from the group

- Building a classroom community begins before school starts.

- What are some ways you prepare for children before they actually begin coming to school?

▶ **Give picture sets or page numbers of illustrations to each group**

- The pictures you will discuss show a variety of ways teachers begin building a sense of community in their classrooms.

- Look through the pictures and generate a list of ideas that you particularly like.

▶ **Pull the group together to share reactions**

- What were your reactions to these pictures?

- What messages would children receive when they enter these classrooms?

- Did they inspire you to think of other ideas for welcoming children to the classroom?

▶ **Introduce the next topic**

- All communities function according to a set of systems that each person agrees to follow.

- The systems you establish in your classroom have to be made explicit to children.

▶ **Generate a list of ideas from the group**

- What are the things you have to introduce to children right from the first day?
  Participants may share ideas such as:
  ◊ *how the room is set up*
  ◊ *where they can find what they need*
  ◊ *the signal for quiet*

▶ **Refer participants to the book**

- On pages 54-56 in *Building the Primary Classroom* you will find suggestions for many of the ideas you mentioned.

Chapter 2 Workshops

WORKSHOP TOPICS	PURPOSE	MATERIALS	APPROXIMATE TIME
Overview	To provide an overview of the content of chapter one.	Notes, overhead, handout p. 48	10-15 minutes
Defining Community (relates to pp. 46-51)	To consider different kinds of communities and how communities have changed.	Notes, overhead handouts, markers chart paper, tape p. 54	20-30 minutes
Welcoming Children to the Classroom (relates to pp. 52-56)	To identify what teachers can do before school and in the first few days to introduce children to the classroom community.	Notes, tape chart, community picture set, paper, markers p. 60	20-30 minutes
How Meetings Build Community (relates to pp. 57-65)	To consider different formats for addressing the whole group and exploring what makes meetings work.	Notes, handout, chart paper, markers p. 64	30-40 minutes
Fostering Meaningful Discussions	To analyze factors that make discussions purposeful and develop plans for conducting meetings.	Notes, two copies of Planning Handout and Meeting Handout p. 70	40-50 minutes

How Meetings Build Community

▶ **Introduce the topic**

- Communication skills—the ability to speak and listen effectively—are central to building a successful classroom community.

- There are many times during the day when teachers want the whole group to hear the same message.

▶ **Distribute Handout, "Addressing the Whole Group"**

- Think of all the times of the day when you address or might address the children as a group. Jot down your ideas at the top of the handout.

▶ **Ask people to share what they wrote and record ideas on a chart**

- Let's create a joint list of the times of the day when you need to talk to everyone.
  Examples from participants may include:
  ◊ *to greet children in the morning*
  ◊ *to give instructions for an activity*
  ◊ *to introduce a new topic of study*
  ◊ *to hear a story*

- There are several different ways you can bring children together as a group.

▶ **Refer back to the handout**

- Three are illustrated on the chart on your handout.

▶ **Have tables count off from 1 to 3**

- Let's count off by tables from 1 to 3.

- Depending on what number you have, look at the setting for that number and jot down your ideas about the message it conveys to children; what children would be doing; and how the setting promotes listening and speaking skills.

- When you are finished, discuss your ideas with others at your table.

- Ask someone at your table to be the reporter and record the major points of your discussion on the handout.

▶ Pull the group together

- Let's take a few minutes to hear from each group. Will the reporters present the suggestions from their groups?

▶ Summarize the key points building on what has been shared

- The first setting is more traditional. Children are expected to keep their eyes on the teacher, to listen, and to raise their hands when they want to speak.

- Setting #2 invites children to talk to one another, to work collaboratively. When the teacher addresses the whole group, however, it may be a less satisfactory arrangement. Children may be distracted by materials or others at their table. To focus on the person talking, some children would have to turn around in their seats.

- Setting #3, a group meeting, conveys that each person is an equally valued member of the classroom community. Each person can share and learn from the others. Everyone can see who is talking and therefore, it is easier to focus and listen.

- Using a meeting format as a way to address the whole group is not something that comes naturally to many teachers. It is, however, an approach that is central to *Building the Primary Classroom*, not only for the purpose of building a sense of community, but as a way of discussing content in all subject areas.

- Running effective meetings requires planning and skill. Teachers must specifically teach children how to talk and listen in a group setting, and how to share and solve problems as a group.

▶ Refer participants to *Building the Primary Classroom*

- In the book on pages 62-65, there are suggestions for running effective meetings.

- On pages 57-62, five different types of meetings are discussed.

- Have half the people at your table read each one of the sections and then share what they learned.

- Think about what you already do in your own classrooms and what new ideas you may want to try.

▶ If you have several days before the next session, give an assignment

- Think about what types of meetings you want to have in your classroom—or how you'd like to improve on the meetings you already have.

- Try having a meeting. It can be brief. Think of an activity such as reading a story and discussing it; talking about what happened on the playground; or giving instructions for an activity.

- Keep notes on what works—and what was less successful. We'll take time to share experiences at the beginning of our next class.

▶ Conclude the session

- Next time we will take a closer look at how a teacher fosters a meaningful discussion during a meeting.

Addressing the Whole Group

Think of all the times of the day when you want all the children in your classroom to hear the same messages.

_____

_____

_____

_____

Three different settings for addressing the whole group are illustrated in the chart below. Jot down your ideas about the message each one conveys, what children are doing, and how each setting promotes listening and speaking skills.

	#1	#2	#3
What are the teacher's goals?			
What are children likely to be doing?			
How does the setting promote listening and speaking skills?			

Chapter 2 Workshops

WORKSHOP TOPICS	PURPOSE	MATERIALS	APPROXIMATE TIME
Overview	To provide an overview of the content of chapter one.	Notes, overhead, handout p. 48	10-15 minutes
Defining Community (relates to pp. 46-51)	To consider different kinds of communities and how communities have changed.	Notes, overhead handouts, markers chart paper, tape p. 54	20-30 minutes
Welcoming Children to the Classroom (relates to pp. 52-56)	To identify what teachers can do before school and in the first few days to introduce children to the classroom community.	Notes, tape chart, community picture set, paper, markers p. 60	20-30 minutes
How Meetings Build Community (relates to pp. 57-65)	To consider different formats for addressing the whole group and exploring what makes meetings work.	Notes, handout, chart paper, markers p. 64	30-40 minutes
Fostering Meaningful Discussions	To analyze factors that make discussions purposeful and develop plans for conducting meetings.	Notes, two copies of Planning Handout and Meeting Handout p. 70	40-50 minutes

Fostering Meaningful Discussions

▶ **Invite participants to share what they have tried (partners, then full class)**

- What sorts of meetings did you have?

- If you were already having meetings (or group time) did you make modifications as a result of what you read?

- What were the results?

▶ **Introduce the topic**

- When children have the skills to talk and listen to others in a meeting, teachers can use the meeting format to hold meaningful discussions.

- Discussions can be on a topic of study in which children share what they know, identify questions to explore, and later share what they are discovering and learning.

- Discussions can also be about an issue related to community life, such as generating a list of jobs for the classroom; identifying rules; resolving a dispute or problem that has come up.

- To identify what makes discussions meaningful, let's analyze a sample discussion. Then I'll ask you to think of other topics you might consider for discussions and have you develop a plan for a meeting you can hold in your own classrooms with children.

▶ **Distribute Handout, "Planning Sheet for a Discussion"**

- This worksheet identifies several steps in conducting a discussion during a meeting.

- First, it's important to do some preplanning. Consider the purpose of the meeting, your goals, and what you need to prepare in terms of materials or resources.

- Next, brainstorm some ways of getting the meeting started—perhaps a list of questions to pose to the group.

- How will you sustain the discussion?

- Finally, how do you plan to conclude the meeting?

▶ Distribute Handout, "A Meeting to Generate Classroom Jobs"

- This handout describes a sample meeting in a second grade classroom.

- Take a few minutes to read it over on your own.* (See note on next page.) Then complete the planning sheet to identify each step Ms. Jeffreys took to conduct the discussion.

- When you have written all you can, take time to share what you wrote with others at your table.

▶ Allow ample time and then bring the group together

- What were your reactions to this meeting?

- Was the discussion purposeful? In what ways?

- Were there aspects of the meeting that you didn't understand or disagreed with?

▶ Distribute a second copy of Planning Handout

- Think about what kinds of discussions you might have with the children in your classroom.

- Find someone who is interested in planning a similar discussion and work together to plan your meeting.

- If you need help, just signal me.

▶ Allow sufficient time for planning, then reconvene and conclude the class

- Over the next week or two, conduct your discussion with the children.

- Keep notes on the results so we can share strategies with one another.

*Note for teacher educators:

Another way to do this activity is to ask for 16 volunteers to choose parts and read the script aloud. If you have more than 16 in the group the extras can be observers. Organize the actors to sit in a circle with the observers on the outside of the circle. When the scene is over debrief together.

Planning Sheet for a Discussion

Purpose of the meeting: _____

_____

Goals: _____

_____

_____

Preparation: _____

_____

_____

Getting the Meeting Started	Sustaining the Discussion	Concluding the Meeting

A Meeting to Generate Classroom Jobs

Ms. Jeffreys, a second grade teacher, is planning a meeting with her class to generate a list of classroom jobs. It's the first week of school and she plans for the meeting carefully, knowing that this type of discussion will be new for many of the children.

Advanced Planning:

Ms. Jeffreys identifies three goals for having classroom jobs:

- To involve as many children as possible at clean up time.

- To have children work in pairs for some jobs in order to help them develop cooperative skills and make new friends.

- To convey to children that the task of identifying classroom jobs is a real problem that deserves careful thinking.

She anticipates that she will have to help the children think about categories, and that they will probably have too many ideas—or, too few.

She writes the following message on a chart:

"Each day we will use this classroom for our work and it will get messy! It is our responsibility to clean it up at the end of each day so that we can easily begin our work the next morning. What jobs do we need to do in order to clean up our room?"

Then she writes a heading on another chart:

"Jobs We Need in Our Classroom"

The Meeting:

Ms. J: "This message tells what we are going to talk about at our meeting today. Let's read it together." (The children read along with Ms. Jeffreys as she points to each word.) "Now, think carefully. Look around the room. Think of all the things we use each day. What will have to be cleaned up at the end of the the day? Let's think of some jobs and list them on our chart."

Lavinia: "The blackboards."

Ms. J: "Yes, Lavinia. We use the blackboards. What job would need to be done to the blackboards?"

Lavinia: "Erase them."

Henry: "Wash them."

Ms. J: "Okay. Should we put Blackboard Washer on the chart?"

The class yells out yes.

Ryan: "Chairs."

Ms. J: "Ryan, what would need to be done to the chairs?"

Ryan shrugs.

Ms. J: "Any ideas about what we would need to do to the chairs?'

Christine: "Push them in?"

Ryan: "Don't they have to go up on the tables?"

Ms. J: "Good thinking, Ryan. Christine, do you agree?"

Christine nods yes. Ms. Jeffreys writes "Chairs" on the chart.

Brendon: "Should someone wipe the tables before the chairs go on them?"

Ms. J: "Do you agree with Brendon?"

The class calls out yes. She writes "Tabletops" on the list.

Ms. J: "What else besides the blackboard, chairs, and tabletops needs to be fixed up at the end of the day?"

Lucy: "Junk needs to be picked up from the floor."

Ms. J: "Good thinking Lucy. Let's think about the floors for a minute. Any other ideas about the floors?"

Jack: "We could wash them."

Tyrone: "The custodian does that."

Jack: "Then we should sweep them to get the junk up."

Ms. J: "Do you think sweeper is a one or two person job?"

Jack: "Two."

Ms. J: "Jack, can you say why you think sweeper is a two person job?"

Jack: "So it goes faster."

Ms. J: "That's probably true. Any other reasons why it might be a two person job?"

Celeste: "In case someone is sick."

Ms. J: "Celeste is making a good point. Let's hold on floors for a minute and consider Celeste's point. What happens if someone with a job is absent?"

Maria: "Last year in our class we had a job called substitute."

Ms. J: "What do you all think about that?"

Heads nod.

Ms. J: "Let's put substitute on our chart. If someone is sick, the substitute will fill in for that job. What do you think Celeste?"

Celeste agrees.

Ms. J: "Let's go back to the floors for a moment. Does any one want to add reasons why it should be a two person job?"

Teresa: "One to sweep and one to pick up the stuff."

Ms. J: "Do we have equipment in our room for that job?"

Cara: "A broom and a dust pan. I saw them hanging on the hook by the door."

Jack: "That's what I meant by it would go faster."

Ms. J: "Good thinking Jack. So do we all agree that floors is a two person job?"

They call out agreement. Ms. Jeffreys records "Floors ?? 2 people."

Ms. J: "Other ideas for jobs? Think about the different materials you use during the school day."

Maria: "Pencils."

Jack: "Paints."

Martin: "Blocks and Legos."

Many children offer ideas for materials; Ms. Jeffreys records several on the chart.

Ms. J: "What do you think? Should we have a job for each material? We have an awful lot of materials in our classroom."

Ryan: "We don't use everything everyday so sometimes people wouldn't have anything to do."

Maria: "It would be too many jobs."

Ms. J: "Could we group the materials together in some way? Who has some ideas about this?"

Janet: "Like stuff we write with?"

Ms. J: "That's one way we could group things—by how we use them. Talk with your neighbor for a moment and see what ideas you can come up with for categories of materials."

She gives them a few minutes to talk with someone next to them. There are lots of conversations.

Ms. J: "Okay. Let's get back together. What ideas did you discuss?"

Cara: "Jenni and I think we should have writing supplies and art."

On the blackboard Ms. Jeffreys writes "writing and art."

Chris: "We think games and books."

Ms. Jeffreys adds these two ideas to the list.

Janet: "The computer area."

Children offer many ideas. The discussion has been going on for about 20 minutes.

Conclusion

Ms. J: "You've come up with great ideas. I think we'll leave the list here—the ideas on the chart and the categories on the board. Think about our list. If you have other ideas during the day, add them. We'll do clean up today without assigned jobs so that you can think some more about what is needed. Tomorrow we'll make final decisions. We will decide which jobs are for one person and which need two."

3

ESTABLISHING A STRUCTURE FOR THE CLASSROOM

Chapter 3 Workshops

WORKSHOP TOPICS	PURPOSE	MATERIALS	APPROXIMATE TIME
Overview	To provide an overview of the content of chapter 3.	Notes, overhead, handout p. 82	5-10 minutes
Types of Structure	To examine three different approaches to classroom structure and how each one impacts on children's behavior.	Notes, handout, chart paper, markers, tape p. 86	40-50 minutes
The Physical Environment (Relates to pp. 102-125)	To identify ways of arranging the classroom environment to help children become self-directed and collaborative learners.	Notes, handout, structure picture set, chart paper, markers, tape p. 90	50-60 minutes
Routines and Rules [Relates to pp. 131-146]	To demonstrate the importance of making the structure clear to children.	Notes, handout, props for skits, markers, paper, scissors, tape p. 96	50-60 minutes
Messages Conveyed by the Structure (Relates to pp. 100-101)	To identify how the environment, schedule and routines, and rules can convey positive messages.	Notes, handout, structure picture set p. 100	20-30 minutes

Overview

▶ Introduce the strategy

- The third strategy of *Building the Primary Classroom* is Establishing a Structure in the Classroom.

- Every community has its own structure—the rules, understandings, and systems that all members agree to follow.

- Without a predictable structure, people often feel insecure and unsafe because they don't know what is expected or how to act appropriately.

- When the structure is clear, it is easier for everyone to work and to feel productive.

▶ Put on overhead and give Handout, "Establishing a Structure for the Classroom"

- This overhead highlights the three components of establishing a structure in the classroom.

- I will give a brief overview of each component. You have this as a handout if you wish to take notes.

▶ Discuss the physical environment

- One source of structure in the classroom is the physical environment itself.

- It includes the type and arrangement of furniture, the types and arrangement of materials and supplies, and how children's physical needs are met.

- When well-organized, the physical environment is an aspect of structure that can support children's independence and their ability to work collaboratively with others.

▶ **Discuss the daily schedule and routines**

- The schedule and routines reflect the way you want children to spend their days.

- A predictable schedule and clearly defined routines give children a sense of order and help them feel safe.

▶ **Discuss clear expectations about behavior**

- Every classroom community needs rules so children know what behavior is acceptable and what will not be tolerated. Equally important is the idea that if we want children to make good decisions about behavior we need to give them opportunites to think about the need for rules and how to apply them.

- Children are more likely to abide by rules and develop self discipline when they have participated in generating the rules. Children need to spend time figuring out what went wrong and why, when rules are broken.

- This last component of establishing structure includes how to involve children in creating classroom rules, sharing responsibility for maintaining the classroom, and ensuring that children use and care for materials properly.

Establishing a Structure for the Classroom

- The Physical Environment

- The Daily Schedule and Routines

- Clear Expectations About Behavior

Chapter 3 Workshops

WORKSHOP TOPICS	PURPOSE	MATERIALS	APPROXIMATE TIME
Overview	To provide an overview of the content of chapter 3.	Notes, overhead, handout p. 82	5-10 minutes
Types of Structure	To examine three different approaches to classroom structure and how each one impacts on children's behavior.	Notes, handout, chart paper, markers, tape p. 86	40-50 minutes
The Physical Environment (Relates to pp. 102-125)	To identify ways of arranging the classroom environment to help children become self-directed and collaborative learners.	Notes, handout, structure picture set, chart paper, markers, tape p. 90	50-60 minutes
Routines and Rules (Relates to pp. 131-146)	To demonstrate the importance of making the structure clear to children.	Notes, handout, props for skits, markers, paper, scissors, tape p. 96	50-60 minutes
Messages Conveyed by the Structure (Relates to pp. 100-101)	To identify how the environment, schedule and routines, and rules can convey positive messages.	Notes, handout, structure picture set p. 100	20-30 minutes

Types of Structure

Note to teacher educators:

The handout for this topic can be read and discussed by participants, or used to plan skits. If used for skits, make a copy of the handout and cut on the dotted line so you can give one section to each group.

▶ Introduce the topic

- All children need structure; and all teachers want structure.

- It is very difficult for teachers to teach effectively, and for children to learn when the structure is not clear.

- The type of structure you create depends on the kind of learners you want children to become.

▶ Divide the groups into three teams

- This activity is designed to allow you to explore different types of classroom structure and what effect each one has on children.

- We're going to need three groups. Each group will receive a description of a different classroom.

- When you have your group together, I'll give you your assignment.

▶ Give one section of the handout to each group

- Find a place where you can sit together and plan a skit to present your classroom setting to the rest of the group.

- Take about 5-10 minutes to plan your skit. Let me know if you need more time.

▶ Reconvene the group and discuss the observation questions written on a chart

- As each group presents a skit, think about the following questions to assess the classroom structure:
  - ◊ In what ways has the structure been established?
  - ◊ Is the structure clear to the children? What are some clues?
  - ◊ What effect does the structure have on children's behavior?

- You may want to jot down some notes to yourself as you observe each presentation.

▶ Have a group discussion about the questions after each skit is presented

- Let's hear your observations.

▶ Summarize the discussion, highlighting key points

- At the beginning of this session I stated that the type of structure you create in the classroom depends on what kind of learners you want children to become.

- In classroom 3, a clear structure has been established, though it may not be obvious at first.

- Children are engaged in tasks that have meaning for them. They can explain what they are doing and why.

- Children know what they are expected to do; they are self-directed.

- The structure is clear to the children because:
  - ◊ they know where to find and return materials and how to use them;
  - ◊ they understand the classroom routines; and
  - ◊ they know the rules.

- Therefore, it's not only important to create the structure itself, but to also make it very clear and explicit to the children.

Different Kinds of Structure

The classrooms described below reflect different approaches to structure.

Classroom 1

Before you enter this classroom you can hear the teacher's voice above the substantial commotion in the classroom. "If you don't get into your seats in 30 seconds, there will be no recess today," calls the teacher from the front of the room. This threat appears to have little effect on the children. Two children continue chasing each other around the room to the applause of a small group of admirers. Several small groups are chatting away in different parts of the room. The rest of the children are either moving around the room, sitting in their seats, stuffing papers in their lockers, or talking to friends. The teacher sighs and says, "I've got all the behavior problems in my class, every last one of them. They curse and fight at the slightest provocation. They have no respect for authority or for anyone or anything. I spend most of my time being a policeman, just trying to keep order. I'm hitting my head against the wall, just waiting for school to be over. If I knew that teaching was going to be like this, I would have tried an easier and more satisfying profession!"

Classroom 2

As you approach this classroom, you wonder if anyone is there because it's so quiet. You enter and find the teacher at her desk checking a child's workbook. The rest of the children are working quietly at individual desks which are lined up in rows. Most of the children are reading or writing in their workbooks. Several children are looking over their neighbor's shoulders, trying to see what they have written. A few are whispering. The teacher looks up, clears her throat loudly and asks, "Do I hear any talking?" This brings immediate quiet. The teacher asks you to watch her children for ten minutes while she makes a phone call to one of the parents. Before leaving the room she tells the children they have ten more minutes to finish their work. About one minute after she leaves, several children are up out of their chairs, rough housing with friends. There's a lively buzz of talking in the room, followed by squeals of laughter when the class clown gets up in front and starts putting on a show. You remind children that they are supposed to be finishing their work quietly, but it has little effect. Chaos reigns until the teacher returns when all the children run for their seats and get back to work.

Classroom 3

When you enter the classroom, you hear a steady hum of activity and talking. At first you don't see the teacher; she is sitting and talking with one of several small groups of children working on a variety of math activities. They are seated at tables arranged in separate sections of the room. Each group has three to four children and they seem intent on the materials they are using together. Children are talking in lively voices about what they are doing, explaining their ideas, giving directions, asking questions, challenging each other, and laughing. You sit down near one group of four children using geoboards and rubber bands. "Tell me something about what you are doing," you say. One child immediately volunteers: "We are finding out how many ways we can make different shapes. Look, we've made triangles, squares, and diamonds," he says, pointing to each one. Another child adds, "And I've made a hexagon. I know because it has six angles and six sides." You then ask, "How did you know what to do?" A third child explains, "We had a meeting and talked about different shapes we knew. Then each group got different things to use. We got the geoboards, that group got popsicle sticks, over there they have tangrams. Look around and you'll see." Just before you leave the teacher calls the children together in the meeting area so the groups can report on what they did and what they learned.

Chapter 3 Workshops

WORKSHOP TOPICS	PURPOSE	MATERIALS	APPROXIMATE TIME
Overview	To provide an overview of the content of chapter 3.	Notes, overhead, handout p. 82	5-10 minutes
Types of Structure	To examine three different approaches to classroom structure and how each one impacts on children's behavior.	Notes, handout, chart paper, markers, tape p. 86	40-50 minutes
The Physical Environment (Relates to pp. 102-125)	**To identify ways of arranging a classroom environment to help children become self-directed and collaborative learners.**	**Notes, handout, structure picture set, chart paper, markers, tape** **p. 90**	**50-60 minutes**
Routines and Rules (Relates to pp. 131-146)	To demonstrate the importance of making the structure clear to children.	Notes, handout, props for skits, markers, paper, scissors, tape p. 96	50-60 minutes
Messages Conveyed by the Structure (Relates to pp. 100-101)	To identify how the environment, schedule and routines, and rules can convey positive messages.	Notes, handout, structure picture set p. 100	20-30 minutes

The Physical Environment

Note to teacher educators:

The second part of this workshop involves participants in examining a variety of classrooms and classroom displays. The purpose is to encourage discussion about the multiple ways the organization of the physical environment helps you to establish a classroom structure that promotes independence and collaboration. Structure is established through the way materials are organized and displayed, how furniture is arranged, and in the systems that are created for using materials and supplies. You can either create your own set of pictures to use or have participants discuss some of the illustrations in *Building the Primary Classroom*. We recommend the following illustrations for discussion:

- Page 99: The arrangement of furniture
- Page 102: Children on benches in a meeting area, cubbies underneath for individual storage
- Page 105: Displays of children's work
- Page 109: Shared writing materials, labeled shelves
- Page 111: Shared math materials, labeled shelves
- Page 117: Procedures for using paint
- Page 118: Block area clean-up and storage systems
- Page 120: Storage of cookin supplies
- Page 121: Computer use directions
- Page 130: Display of the daily schedule
- Page 137: A choice board system
- Page 141: A list of rules
- Page 144: A list of classroom jobs
- Page 330: Small group work at a table
- Page 336: Small group work at a table
- Page 361: Display of ongoing research by children

▶ Introduce the topic

- The physical environment of a classroom—the arrangement of furniture and the selection and display of materials—has a profound effect on children.

- Classroom arrangement is one of the most powerful ways to create a clear structure.

- To examine the impact of the physical environment, think for a moment about a store where you hate to shop. Picture yourself in that store, trying to find what you need and get out as soon as possible. Think about what it feels like to shop there.

- What is it about the store that frustrates you?

▶ **Distribute Handout, "Stores Where I Hate to Shop" for individual use**

- In the left hand column of this handout, jot down the characteristics of the store that came to mind, the ones that make the store an unpleasant, difficult place to shop. Put a characteristic in each space.

- When you have identified the frustrating characteristics, take a few minutes to reflect on how each characteristic affects you—both your behavior and how you feel.

▶ **Invite participants to share at their tables, then in the large group**

- When you are finished, talk to the people at your table about your experiences.

- Did any common themes emerge from your discussion?

- Do any of these characteristics also apply to the classroom?

▶ **Give the next instructions**

- The last column on your page is blank. In the handout, write the following: "How These Characteristics Affect Children in the Classroom."

- Take a few minutes to reflect on this statement and record the ideas that come to mind.

▶ **Invite participants to share their ideas**

- It's pretty evident that you saw a number of similarities between classroom arrangement and frustrating stores.

- What affect would poor arrangements have on children?

- Let's recall some real life examples.

- Just as the physical environment can have a negative effect, it can also be organized in ways that support our goals for children.

▶ Give picture sets to each group or list page numbers of illustrations in the book

- Let's consider two goals: to help children learn to function independently in the classroom and to encourage them to work collaboratively with others.

- Take some time to study and discuss the pictures at your table.

- Ask someone to be a recorder and take notes on your group's discussion of how the physical environment of these classrooms helps teachers achieve these goals.

▶ Allow approximately 15 minutes before calling on each group to report

- In reporting on your discussion, let's have the reporters take turns giving one idea at a time for their groups, until we have heard everything each group discussed.

▶ Prepare charts: 1) Independence and Self-Direction, 2) Collaboration

- I've put up two charts. On one we'll list ways in which the environment helps children develop independence and self-direction. On the second we'll list how the environment supports children in working collaboratively.

▶ Summarize the discussion and refer participants to *Building the Primary Classroom*

- Many of the ideas you identified are discussed in detail on pages 102-125 in your book. (**Note to teacher educators**: If you are working with teachers rather than preservice students you may want to suggest this follow-up activity.) Over the next week, read through these pages and try out some of the ideas you like.

- Keep a record of what you do and how the changes affect the children.

Stores Where I Hate to Shop

Characteristics of Stores Where I Hate to Shop	How These Characteristics Affect Me	

Chapter 3 Workshops

WORKSHOP TOPICS	PURPOSE	MATERIALS	APPROXIMATE TIME
Overview	To provide an overview of the content of chapter 3.	Notes, overhead, handout p. 82	5-10 minutes
Types of Structure	To examine three different approaches to classroom structure and how each one impacts on children's behavior.	Notes, handout, chart paper, markers, tape p. 86	40-50 minutes
The Physical Environment (Relates to pp. 102-125)	To identify ways of arranging the classroom environment to help children become self-directed and collaborative learners.	Notes, handout, structure picture set, chart paper, markers, tape p. 90	50-60 minutes
Routines and Rules (Relates to pp. 131-146)	To demonstrate the importance of making the structure clear to children.	Notes, handout, props for skits, markers, paper, scissors, tape p. 96	50-60 minutes
Messages Conveyed by the Structure (Relates to pp. 100-101)	To identify how the environment, schedule and routines, and rules can convey positive messages.	Notes, handout, structure picture set p. 100	20-30 minutes

Routines and Rules

Note to teacher educators:
If possible, arrange for separate rooms/spaces where small groups can work to prepare their demonstrations.

▶ **Introduce the topics**

- The routines and rules you have for your classroom make it a predictable and safe place for children.

- Routines are procedures that ensure the effective use of time and space.

- Routines will differ from one classroom to the next. They become part of the culture of your classroom.

- You'll often hear children say "This is our way of doing things."

- Classroom rules are also part of the classroom structure. Children feel safer when they know how they are expected to behave, and when rules are consistently enforced.

▶ **Divide the group into four teams of four to eight people in each group**

- We're going to count off by 4's so we can form teams.

- Please find a place/table where your team can meet.

- I've prepared assignment cards for each team that I will distribute.

- After you've had a chance to read through the assigned pages in *Building the Primary Classroom*, discuss what you read with the members of your team.

- Plan a way to present the information to the rest of the group. It can be a skit, an activity that involves the whole group, or anything that will most effectively convey the ideas. Plan for 2-4 minutes each.

- Take 20 minutes to read, discuss, and prepare your presentation.

▶ Allow 20-30 minutes for the demonstrations and follow-up discussions

- I have set out some materials and props if you need them.

- Let me know if I can help in any way or if you need anything you don't see on the table.

Assignment Cards

Note to teacher educators:

Duplicate this handout, then cut along the dotted lines so you can give each team one assignment.

Teaching Routines to Children

1. Read page 131-135 in *Building the Primary Classroom* on "Establishing Classroom Routines."
2. Discuss what you read and how you establish and teach routines in your classrooms.
3. Decide on a way to demonstrate how a teacher could teach routines to children.

Teaching Children to Make Choices

1. Read pages 135-138 in *Building the Primary Classroom* on "Offering Children Choices."
2. Discuss what you read and how you offer children choices in your classrooms.
3. Plan a way to present this information to the group.

Generating Rules With Children

1. Read pages 139-142 in *Building the Primary Classroom* on "Involving Children in Creating Classroom Rules."
2. Discuss how you developed rules in your classrooms and what rules you have.
3. Decide on a way to demonstrate how a teacher would involve children in developing rules for the classroom.

Introducing Materials

1. Read pages 145-147 in *Building the Primary Classroom* on "Introducing the Proper Use of Materials."
2. Discuss how you introduce materials to children in your classrooms.
3. Decide on a way to demonstrate how a teacher might introduce materials to a group of children. You can use any of the props you need.

Chapter 3 Workshops

WORKSHOP TOPICS	PURPOSE	MATERIALS	APPROXIMATE TIME
Overview	To provide an overview of the content of chapter 3.	Notes, overhead, handout p. 82	5-10 minutes
Types of Structure	To examine three different approaches to classroom structure and how each one impacts on children's behavior.	Notes, handout, chart paper, markers, tape p. 86	40-50 minutes
The Physical Environment (Relates to pp. 102-125)	To identify ways of arranging the classroom environment to help children become self-directed and collaborative learners.	Notes, handout, structure picture set, chart paper, markers, tape p. 90	50-60 minutes
Routines and Rules (Relates to pp. 131-146)	To demonstrate the importance of making the structure clear to children.	Notes, handout, props for skits markers, paper, scissors, tape p. 96	50-60 minutes
Messages Conveyed by the Structure (Relates to pp. 100-101)	To identify how the environment, schedule and routines, and rules can convey positive messages.	Notes, handout, structure picture set p. 100	20-30 minutes

Messages Conveyed by the Structure

▷ **Distribute Handout, "Positive Messages Conveyed by the Classroom Structure"**

- In previous workshops we discussed a wide variety of ways to create a clear and consistent structure in the classroom.

- As a way of summarizing what we have done, and looking at structure from a different perspective, this handout asks you to identify ways that the environment, structure and routines, and clear expectations about behavior can convey four distinct messages to children.

▷ **Have each table select a different message**

- Look over the messages on the handout and select one that you want to focus on. I want to be sure each message is covered so let me know when you've decided.

- After you have agreed upon the message you will discuss, list all the ways teachers can convey this message.

▷ **Distribute picture sets to each table or refer back to page numbers of illustrations**

- You can use the pictues sets (or illustrations) we discussed previously to refer to if you like. Please don't feel confined by the pictures—generate your own ideas with the people at your table.

▷ **Reconvene the group and ask each table to report. Then summarize**

- You may have already noticed that some of the messages are similar to the ones on pages 100-101 in *Building the Primary Classroom.*

- Look at the chart in the book and see if there are any ideas you want to add to your handout.

- As you try some of these ideas on structure, keep notes in a journal on how children respond to the changes you make.

Positive Messages Conveyed
by the Classroom Structure

Use the chart below to think of ways the classroom structure can convey positive messages to children.

Positive Messages	The Physical Environment	The Daily Schedule and Routine	Clear Expectations About Behavior
"You will feel safe, cared-for, and respected here."			
"You are an important member of the group."			
"There will be interesting things to study, investigate, and learn about."			
"You will find what you need and make choices."			

4

GUIDING
CHILDREN'S
LEARNING

Chapter 4 Workshops

WORKSHOP TOPICS	PURPOSE	MATERIALS	APPROXIMATE TIME
Overview	To provide an overview of the content of chapter 4.	Notes, overhead, handout p. 106	5-10 minutes
Making Learning Meaningful	To show how an activity can engage children in meaningful learning.	Notes, chart paper, markers for each table p. 112	30-40 minutes
Helping Children Construct Knowledge (Relates to pp. 150-152)	To consider how teachers can create opportunities for children to actively construct knowledge.	Notes, handout, chart paper and markers p. 116	20-30 minutes
Stages in the Learning Process (Relates to pp. 155-158)	To identify ways teachers can enrich children's experiences at each stage in the learning process.	Notes, handout p. 120	20-30 minutes
Investigation, Representation, Reflection (Relates to pp. 166-171)	To consider how work times and long-term studies can be designed to guide children's learning.	Notes, handouts p. 124	30-45 minutes
A Learning Community	To explore how the first three strategies provide the foundation for guiding children's learning.	Notes, picture set p. 130	25-35 minutes
Generating Ideas for Long-Term Studies (Relates to pp. 172-181)	To demonstrate a process for thinking about study topics.	Notes, markers, small pieces of paper, chart paper p. 134	20-30 minutes
Planning a Long-Term Study	To generate initial plans for a study using a step-by-step process.	Notes, handouts, small pieces of paper p. 138	60-75 minutes

Overview

Note to teacher educators:

This information can be presented as a mini-lecture in an introduction to the strategy or as part of the Workshop, "Making Learning Meaningful," to summarize the activity.

▶ Introduce the strategy

- All teachers want children to become confident, competent learners.

- A competent learner understands the processes of learning: how to define a problem, find needed information, put ideas together in an organized way, and apply knowledge to new situations.

- The early elementary years establish a foundation for life-long learning. Therefore, how teachers guide children's learning is as important as what children learn.

- The fourth strategy for building the primary classroom describes the teacher's role as a guide in the learning process.

▶ Put on overhead

- This overhead highlights what teachers need to know, think about, and plan for to facilitate guiding children's learning.

- I will give an overview of what is addressed in each section. You have this as a handout if you wish to take notes.

▶ Discuss how children learn

- Effective teachers base their decisions on a philosophy of education that is responsive to the needs and interests of children. This philosophy comes from the work of learning theorists and psychologists as well as our own experiences working with children.

- I will highlight four central concepts about how children learn.
  - ◊ Children **construct knowledge**. They explore the world around them to learn how things work. To learn something new, they begin with the familiar. In the process of experimenting and interacting with materials, they connect new information to what they already know.

  - ◊ Learning is a **social experience**. When children have opportunities to work with their peers to solve problems, they are exposed to the ideas of others, share their understandings, and achieve new insights.

  - ◊ Children **learn through play** that is productive and purposeful. In the primary grades, play may involve making discoveries with pattern blocks, scales, or magnifying glass, using blocks to construct a map of the neighborhood around the school; dramatizing stories, and learning the rules of a game that requires dice-rolling and score-keeping.

  - ◊ Learning takes place in **stages**. Children move from a concrete, personal understanding to a symbolic, and more conventional one. For young children, content should relate to their own experiences so that they can make connections with what they already know.

Discuss principles that guide teachers in planning

- Teachers constantly make decisions as they plan how to teach the curriculum. Some are made in advance, some are made on-the-spot; they may be about teaching a specific skill or introducing a long-term project. Four principles can guide teachers' planning.

- The first principle is that **learning should be purposeful and relevant** to children's lives. Purposeful learning recognizes that when we have a reason and a desire to find something out, our willingness to learn increases.

- The second principle is that **meaningful learning is integrated**. Integrated curriculum means planning activities that enable children to gain knowledge and apply skills across many discipines. When children are encouraged to write and talk about stories or math problems, they are naturally integrating curriculum. Teachers make their planning and scheduling easier when they find ways to integrate curriculum.

- The third principle is that **communication is central to learning**. Putting ideas into words to explain them to others clarifies thinking. When teachers ask open-ended questions, they encourage children to think about many possible answers and to reflect on what they know.

- The fourth and last principle is **learning takes time**. An effective daily schedule provides extended work times of 45 minutes to an hour to allow children to get involved in an activity. Teachers can model "thinking time"—taking time to think before responding or beginning a project—to show children that quick responses aren't always required.

▶ Discuss ways children construct knowledge

- **Investigation**, **representation**, and **reflection** are the three ways children develop understanding by contructing knowledge.

- Teachers provide opportunities for children to investigate a problem, represent their thinking in a variety of ways, and reflect on what they are learning and how.

▶ Discuss organizing the curriculum

- How do teachers apply these principles about guiding children's learning to address curriculum guidelines and standards?

- Teachers need a plan.

- *Building the Primary Classroom* shows how teachers plan long-term studies, schedule daily work times, and use "teachable moments" to address content and skills in all curriculum subjects.

Guiding Children's Learning

- How Children Learn

- Principles That Guide Teachers in Planning

- Ways Children Construct Knowledge

- Organizing the Curriculum

Chapter 4 Workshops

WORKSHOP TOPICS	PURPOSE	MATERIALS	APPROXIMATE TIME
Overview	To provide an overview of the content of chapter 4.	Notes, overhead, handout p. 106	5-10 minutes
Making Learning Meaningful	To show how an activity can engage children in meaningful learning.	Notes, chart paper, markers for each table p. 112	30-40 minutes
Helping Children Construct Knowledge (Relates to pp. 150-152)	To consider how teachers can create opportunities for children to actively construct knowledge.	Notes, handout, chart paper and markers p. 116	20-30 minutes
Stages in the Learning Process (Relates to pp. 155-158)	To identify ways teachers can enrich children's experiences at each stage in the learning process.	Notes, handout p. 120	20-30 minutes
Investigation, Representation, Reflection (Relates to pp. 166-171)	To consider how work times and long-term studies can be designed to guide children's learning.	Notes, handouts , p. 124	30-45 minutes
A Learning Community	To explore how the first three strategies provide the foundation for guiding children's learning.	Notes, picture set p. 130	25-35 minutes
Generating Ideas for Long-Term Studies (Relates to pp. 172-181)	To demonstrate a process for thinking about study topics.	Notes, markers, small pieces of paper, chart paper p. 134	20-30 minutes
Planning a Long-Term Study	To generate initial plans for a study using a step-by-step process.	Notes, handouts, small pieces of paper p. 138	60-75 minutes

Making Learning Meaningful

▶ **Introduce the activity**

- We are going to do an activity to highlight the underlying principles of making learning meaningful for children.

▶ **Give instructions**

- Each table will work together as a group.

- Please select any five objects from your pockets or pocketbook and place them on the table. You will get them back!

- Take some time to examine the set of objects.

- Talk with the people at your table about different ways you could organize them.

▶ **Allow about 5 minutes, then give the next instruction**

- Now, as a group, decide on one way of organizing your objects.

- Your next task is to come up with a way to represent how your group organized the objects so you can share it with the rest of us.

- Chart paper and markers are available should you need them but don't feel you have to use them. (If you feel a group needs some ideas you can suggest a chart, graph, or diagram of some kind; a song, poem, or skit; or a drawing or construction.)

▶ **Allow about 15 minutes and then reconvene the whole group**

• Let's take some time to share your representations. Which group would like to present first?

▶ **After everyone has shared give this instruction**

• Take a few minutes to write some notes to yourself about how your group functioned, what you learned from other members of your group, and what you learned from the work of the other groups.

▶ **Debrief this reflection**

• Let's share your reflections.
   Participants' ideas may include the following:
   ◊ *Everyone participated.*
   ◊ *A leader emerged.*
   ◊ *One person had an idea and then each of us added onto it.*
   ◊ *I learned about something I wouldn't have thought of on my own.*
   ◊ *Other groups did things we didn't think of at all.*

▶ **Apply the experience to work with children**

• Think about why an activity like this, designed for children, might be successful.

• The activity we just did addresses what we know about how children learn:
   ◊ Children construct knowledge.
   ◊ Learning is a social experience.
   ◊ Play engages children in active learning.
   ◊ Learning takes place in stages.

▶ **Solicit ideas from the group and then summarize**

• The activity incorporates the four principles that guide teachers in planning for children's learning.
   ◊ Learning should be purposeful and relevant.
   ◊ Meaningful learning is integrated.
   ◊ Communication is central to learning.
   ◊ Learning takes time.

- Finally, the activity involved you in your own understanding of information.
  ◊ You actively investigated the objects.
  ◊ You found different ways to represent what you did with the objects and you learned from seeing the way others did it.
  ◊ You reflected on the experience—how your group worked, how you participated, and what you learned from the activity.

▶ **Give instructions for jigsaw reading**

- Please form teams of four.

- On pages 159-165 in *Building the Primary Classroom*, the four principles for guiding children's learning are discussed.

- Have one person read each section and reflect on how the activity we just did relates to that section.

- Share your reactions to the section with the three other members of your reading group.

Chapter 4 Workshops

WORKSHOP TOPICS	PURPOSE	MATERIALS	APPROXIMATE TIME
Overview	To provide an overview of the content of chapter 4.	Notes, overhead, handout p. 106	5-10 minutes
Making Learning Meaningful	To show how an activity can engage children in meaningful learning.	Notes, chart paper, markers for each table p. 112	30-40 minutes
Helping Children Construct Knowledge (Relates to pp. 150-152)	To consider how teachers can create opportunities for children to actively construct knowledge.	Notes, handout, chart paper and markers p. 116	20-30 minutes
Stages in the Learning Process (Relates to pp. 155-158)	To identify ways teachers can enrich children's experiences at each stage in the learning process.	Notes, handout p. 120	20-30 minutes
Investigation, Representation, Reflection (Relates to pp. 166-171)	To consider how work times and long-term studies can be designed to guide children's learning.	Notes, handouts p. 124	30-45 minutes
A Learning Community	To explore how the first three strategies provide the foundation for guiding children's learning.	Notes, picture set p. 130	25-35 minutes
Generating Ideas for Long-Term Studies (Relates to pp. 172-181)	To demonstrate a process for thinking about study topics.	Notes, markers, small pieces of paper, chart paper p. 134	20-30 minutes
Planning a Long-Term Study	To generate initial plans for a study using a step-by-step process.	Notes, handouts, small pieces of paper p. 138	60-75 minutes

Helping Children Construct Knowledge

▶ **Introduce the topic**

- Children learn by constructing their own understandings with the support and guidance offered by a teacher.

- They benefit from opportunities to explore and figure out how and why things work.

- They like to use all their senses in exploring and investigating.

- Children need many opportunities to form explanations based on experiences and to revise those explanations as they learn more.

▶ **Introduce the activity**

- We are going to read about an actual classroom situation where a child developed his own theories about scientific phenomenon, and consider how a teacher might guide further learning.

▶ **Distribute the Handout, "Helping Children Construct Knowledge"**

- Take 5-10 minutes to read the example and reflect on the questions.

- Brainstorm with the people at your table about how you might respond to help this child construct knowledge.

▶ **Reconvene the group**

- Let's take a few minutes to share what you discussed.

- What examples did you think of for your own classroom?

Helping Children Construct Knowledge

Six-year-old Petey looks at the fish tank in the classroom and announces, "We have to put more water in the fish tank because the fish are drinking the water." His teacher asks how he knows this is happening, and Petey replies, "Two reasons. First, they keep opening and closing their mouths. And second, the water used to be up to here (pointing to the water line at the top of the fish tank) and now it's down here" (pointing to the current level).

1. How is Petey attempting to construct knowledge?

2. Identify some ways you might respond to Petey.

3. What experiences might you plan to allow Petey to explore his theories further?

4. Think of an example from your own classroom where a child came up with an explanation for an event. Describe what happened.

Chapter 4 Workshops

WORKSHOP TOPICS	PURPOSE	MATERIALS	APPROXIMATE TIME
Overview	To provide an overview of the content of chapter 4.	Notes, overhead, handout p. 106	5-10 minutes
Making Learning Meaningful	To show how an activity can engage children in meaningful learning.	Notes, chart paper, markers for each table p. 112	30-40 minutes
Helping Children Construct Knowledge (Relates to pp. 150-152)	To consider how teachers can create opportunities for children to actively construct knowledge.	Notes, handout, chart paper and markers p. 116	20-30 minutes
Stages in the Learning Process (relates to pp. 155-158)	To identify ways teachers can enrich children's experiences at each stage in the learning process.	Notes, handout p. 120	20-30 minutes
Investigation, Representation, Reflection (Relates to pp. 166-171)	To consider how work times and long-term studies can be designed to guide children's learning.	Notes, handouts, p. 124	30-45 minutes
A Learning Community	To explore how the first three strategies provide the foundation for guiding children's learning.	Notes, picture set p. 130	25-35 minutes
Generating Ideas for Long-Term Studies (Relates to pp. 172-181)	To demonstrate a process for thinking about study topics.	Notes, markers, small pieces of paper, chart paper p. 134	20-30 minutes
Planning a Long-Term Study	To generate initial plans for a study using a step-by-step process.	Notes, handouts, small pieces of paper p. 138	60-75 minutes

Stages in the Learning Process

▶ **Introduce the topic**

- In the book *Reaching Potentials* (NAEYC, 1992), the authors Bredekamp and Rosegrant, describe learning as a four-stage process.

- The four stages are awareness, exploration, inquiry, and utilization.

- Teachers plan for children's learning depending on where children are in the learning process. Let's take learning to read as an example.

- At the first stage, **awareness**, teachers fill the room with books and read to children daily to foster their interest in reading. They record children's words and post signs in the room.

- At the second stage, **exploration**, teachers want children to begin to explore books. Again, teachers encourage this by supporting children when they "pretend" read and tell the story using picture cues.

- In the third stage, **inquiry**, children are ready to learn conventional strategies. This is when teachers directly teach skills and strategies in reading.

- At the stage of **utilization**, children have acquired a new skill and they want to use it. At this stage teachers make sure there are books available at the appropriate level to enable children to use and refine what they have learned.

▶ **Introduce the activity**

- We are going to do an activity. Please work with a partner.

- This activity is designed to help you to think about how to meet the needs of children who are at varying stages in the learning process, no matter what skill or topic is under investigation.

▶ Introduce the Handout, "Stages in the Learning Process"

- Work with your partner using the handout. Consider how you might address children's needs at each of the four stages of learning to use writing to express ideas.

▶ Refer participants to *Building the Primary Classroom*

- You may want to refer to pages 155-158 of the book to help you generate your ideas.

▶ Call the groups back to share

- There are many ways to provide rich experiences for children at each stage of the learning process.

- What ideas did you come up with?
  Participants may have suggestions such as the following:
  ◊ Awareness
  > *Call attention to notes you write to the office or to other teachers.*
  > *Make writing tools available in the classroom.*
  > *Have labels and signs throughout the room using pictures and words.*
  ◊ Exploration
  > *Have a message board in the classroom and write notes to the children and encourage them to write to you and each other.*
  > *Give children journal books and encourage writing and pictures.*
  > *Have children "read" their writing to you and each other.*
  > *Encourage invented or phonetic spelling.*
  ◊ Inquiry
  > *Keep records of children's progress as writers so you know when to teach particular skills.*
  > *When children are ready, have them keep a personal spelling dictionary of words they are learning to spell correctly.*
  > *Have resources available around the room of words children need for their writing.*
  > *Encourage children to refer to their reading books as a resource for standard writing.*
  ◊ Utilization
  > *Provide opportunities for children to write for a purpose: letters requesting information, thank you notes, reports, signs, instructions.*
  > *Have children make the signs and labels for the classroom.*

Stages in the Learning Process

Describe how you could provide appropriate experiences for children at each stage in the process of learning about writing. (*Reaching Potentials*, NAEYC, 1992).

Awareness: How will I encourage children to become aware of writing?

Exploration: What will I do to help children to explore writing on their own?

Inquiry: How will I know when children are ready to learn conventional ways of writing and when they are ready to learn more? What will I do to encourage this?

Utilization: How will I provide opportunities for children to use what they know in meaningful ways?

Chapter 4 Workshops

WORKSHOP TOPICS	PURPOSE	MATERIALS	APPROXIMATE TIME
Overview	To provide an overview of the content of chapter 4.	Notes, overhead, handout p. 106	5-10 minutes
Making Learning Meaningful	To show how an activity can engage children in meaningful learning.	Notes, chart paper, markers for each table p. 112	30-40 minutes
Helping Children Construct Knowledge (Relates to pp. 150-152)	To consider how teachers can create opportunities for children to actively construct knowledge.	Notes, handout, chart paper and markers p. 116	20-30 minutes
Stages in the Learning Process (Relates to pp. 155-158)	To identify ways teachers can enrich children's experiences at each stage in the learning process.	Notes, handout p. 120	20-30 minutes
Investigation, Representation, Reflection (relates to pp. 166-171	To consider how work times and long-term studies can be designed to guide children's learning.	Notes, handouts p. 124	30-45 minutes
A Learning Community	To explore how the first three strategies provide the foundation for guiding children's learning.	Notes, picture set p. 130	25-35 minutes
Generating Ideas for Long-Term Studies (Relates to pp. 172-181)	To demonstrate a process for thinking about study topics.	Notes, markers, small pieces of paper, chart paper p. 134	20-30 minutes
Planning a Long-Term Study	To generate initial plans for a study using a step-by-step process.	Notes, handouts, small pieces of paper p. 138	60-75 minutes

Investigation, Representation, Reflection

▶ **Introduce the topic**

- Teachers plan experiences that allow children to actively investigate a problem, represent their thinking, and reflect on what they are learning.

▶ **Solicit ideas from the group**

- When you think about investigation experiences, what might children be able to do?
  Participants' ideas may include the following:
  ◊ *observe objects, events*
  ◊ *pose questions*
  ◊ *explore materials*
  ◊ *conduct interviews*
  ◊ *have discussions*
  ◊ *read books*
  ◊ *take trips*
  ◊ *create experiments*

- Work with the people at your table to generate a list of ways children could represent what they discover through their investigations.

▶ **Pull the group together to share ideas**

- What were some of your ideas?
  Participants may suggest:
  ◊ *drawings, paintings*
  ◊ *writing*
  ◊ *constructions*
  ◊ *models*
  ◊ *skits*
  ◊ *graphs*
  ◊ *songs*
  ◊ *dances*
  ◊ *puppets*

- Reflection involves stepping back and thinking about what has been learned and what the process was like.

- Teachers help children learn to reflect by encouraging them to consider questions such as the following:
  ◊ What did I learn?
  ◊ What do I know now that I didn't know before?
  ◊ What questions do I have?
  ◊ What do I think about my work?

- Teachers have to think of how and when to build reflection into the work of the classroom.

▶ Distribute Handout, "Using Geoboards"

- We are going to do an activity. Please work with the group of people at your table.

- This handout, "Using Geoboards: A Math Work Time" shows how two different teachers designed a math work time. Please read the handout.

▶ Give participants time to read. When they are ready, proceed

- Discuss at your table each example. Consider the role of investigation, representation, and reflection in each. Imagine what children are actually doing and what the next step might be.

▶ Reconvene the group and invite them to share ideas

- Would anyone like to share some of the ideas discussed at your table?
  Participants may suggest:
  ◊ In Ms. Smith's class:
  The children can explore more.
  The ones who know simple shapes can make complex ones.
  Everyone can be learning different things.
  They won't get bored.

◊ In Ms. Carter's class:
The children who know it will get bored.
It's a hands-on lesson.

- Is there a time when Ms. Carter's approach might be appropriate?
  Participants may suggest:
  When you want to find out which children know how to make a triangle and square.
  After you have conducted a lesson like Ms. Smith's and you want to teach a small group directly about specific shapes.

▶ Distribute Handout, "A Study on Immigration"

- This second handout describes a study on immigration.

- Consider how the concepts of investigation, representation, and reflection can guide a social studies project that will extend over some time.

▶ Reconvene the group to share ideas

- What thoughts do you have about these two different ways of approaching a study of immigration?

▶ Summarize the session

- Awareness of the importance of investigation, representation, and reflection encourages teachers to plan lessons and projects that allow children to be active participants in the learning process.

Using Geoboards: A Math Work Time

In the two examples that follow, teachers use geoboards so that children can explore concepts in geometry.

Ms. Carter, a second grade teacher, shows the children how to construct triangles and squares using rubber bands and a geoboard. Then she has children practice making triangles and squares of different sizes on their geoboards following the instructions she has written on task sheets.

Ms. Smith introduces geoboards and rubber bands to her second grade class. They discuss the attributes of the materials and how to use them carefully. She assigns the following: "Work with a partner to see how many shapes you can make and how many different ways you can construct them. Keep a record of the shapes you make in your math log."

Ms. Carter's Class	Ms. Smith's Class

A Study on Immigration

In the two examples that follow, the teachers take different approaches to a social studies project.

Ms. Jones' third grade class studies immigration using their social studies textbook as the primary source of information. The chapter they read describes the reasons people leave their homelands to move to a new place. The children answer questions at the end of the chapter. Ms. Jones suggests that the children draw pictures of something they remember from the chapter.

Mr. Hernandez begins the study of immigration with his third graders by reading <u>Letters from Rivka</u> by Karen Hesse, a story about a family who leaves their homeland. He encourages the children to tell and write personal stories about moving to a new house, going to a different school, and moving to a new city, state or country. Knowing that many of the children's parents and grandparents were born in different countries, Mr. Hernandez asks the children to think about people they know who are "experts" on the subject of moving from a birth place. The children decide to interview people in the community, including family members, who immigrated to the United States. They form small groups to plan interview questions.

Ms. Jones' Class	Mr. Hernandez's Class

Chapter 4 Workshops

WORKSHOP TOPICS	PURPOSE	MATERIALS	APPROXIMATE TIME
Overview	To provide an overview of the content of chapter 4.	Notes, overhead, handout p. 106	5-10 minutes
Making Learning Meaningful	To show how an activity can engage children in meaningful learning.	Notes, chart paper, markers for each table p. 112	30-40 minutes
Helping Children Construct Knowledge (Relates to pp. 150-152)	To consider how teachers can create opportunities for children to actively construct knowledge.	Notes, handout, chart paper and markers p. 116	20-30 minutes
Stages in the Learning Process (Relates to pp. 155-158)	To identify ways teachers can enrich children's experiences at each stage in the learning process.	Notes, handout p. 120	20-30 minutes
Investigation, Representation, Reflection (Relates to pp. 166-171)	To consider how work times and long-term studies can be designed to guide children's learning.	Notes, handouts, p. 124	30-45 minutes
A Learning Community	To explore how the first three strategies provide the foundation for guiding children's learning.	Notes, picture set p. 130	25-35 minutes
Generating Ideas for Long-Term Studies (Relates to pp.	To demonstrate a process for thinking about study topics.	Notes, markers, small pieces of paper, chart paper p. 134	20-30 minutes 172-181)
Planning a Long-Term Study	To generate initial plans for a study using a step-by-step process.	Notes, handouts, small pieces of paper p. 138	60-75 minutes

A Learning Community

Note to teacher educators:

The content in this workshop is based on the assumption that you have discussed the first three strategies (Knowing Children, Community, and Structure). This workshop involves particpants in examining a variety of pictures of classroom scenes to examine how implementing the first three strategies enables a teacher to guide learning through investigation, representation, and reflection. You can either create your own set of pictures to use or have participants discuss some of the illustrations in *Building the Primary Classroom*.

We recommend the following illustrations for discussion:
- Page 169: Shared materials
- Page 263: Displays that involve children
- Page 288: Teacher working with snall group
- Page 294: Children at work at a table
- Page 330: Teacher working with small group
- Page 336: Children playing a math game
- Page 351: Children's questions about fishing
- Page 361: Children's questions about a Park and discoveries
- Page 381: A record of children's observations
- Page 389: Science and math tools
- Page 409: Children building together

▶ Introduce the topic

- In order to be able to guide children's learning in the ways we've discussed in the previous activities, teachers create a learning community in the classroom.

- The framework for *Building the Primary Classroom* on page 7 of your book identifies three of the strategies we have explored in our sessions: knowing the children you teach, building a classroom community, and establishing a structure for the classroom.

- We are going to do an activity that will show how, with these three strategies in place, teachers can plan experiences that allow children to construct knowledge through investigation, representation, and reflection.

▶ **Give picture sets to each group or list page numbers of illustrations in book**

- Each table will examine some pictures. Take time to review and talk about what is happening in these classrooms.

- What did the teacher know about the children related to their developmental stages, their individual interests, or their culture?

- What do the pictures reflect about the community that has been created, about collaboration, about meetings?

- What about the physical environment, schedules and routines, and expectations for behavior made these experiences possible?

- Ask someone to be a recorder and take notes on your group's observations and discussion.

▶ **Allow approximately 15 minutes before calling on each group to report**

- In reporting on your discussion, let's have the reporters take turns giving one idea at a time for their groups, until we have heard everything each group discussed.

▶ **Meanwhile, prepare 3 charts with the strategies named at the top**

- I've put up 3 charts. Each identifies one strategy. As you make your reports, I'll put your ideas on the chart according to the strategy it reflects.

▶ **Summarize the discussion**

- Think about the points you made as you read through the content chapters of the book.

- Knowing your children helps you plan where to begin, which materials to choose, and what questions to ask.

- The classroom community you create enables children to work in small groups, to share supplies, and to feel safe taking risks.

- The structure you establish enables children to work independently because they know how to use their time, understand classroom rules, and know how to find, use and put away materials.

Chapter 4 Workshops

WORKSHOP TOPICS	PURPOSE	MATERIALS	APPROXIMATE TIME
Overview	To provide an overview of the content of chapter 4.	Notes, overhead, handout p. 106	5-10 minutes
Making Learning Meaningful	To show how an activity can engage children in meaningful learning.	Notes, chart paper, markers for each table p. 112	30-40 minutes
Helping Children Construct Knowledge (Relates to pp. 150-152)	To consider how teachers can create opportunities for children to actively construct knowledge.	Notes, handout, chart paper and markers p. 116	20-30 minutes
Stages in the Learning Process (Relates to pp. 155-158)	To identify ways teachers can enrich children's experiences at each stage in the learning process.	Notes, handout p. 120	20-30 minutes
Investigation, Representation, Reflection (Relates to pp. 166-171)	To consider how work times and long-term studies can be designed to guide children's learning.	Notes, handouts , p. 124	30-45 minutes
A Learning Community	To explore how the first three strategies provide the foundation for guiding children's learning.	Notes, picture set p. 130	25-35 minutes
Generating Ideas for Long-Term Studies (Relates to pp. 172-181)	To demonstrate a process for thinking about study topics.	Notes, markers, small pieces of paper, chart paper p. 134	20-30 minutes
Planning a Long-Term Study	To generate initial plans for a study using a step-by-step process.	Notes, handouts, small pieces of paper p. 138	60-75 minutes

Generating Ideas for Long-Term Studies

▶ Introduce the topic

- We are going to go through a process that will demonstrate a collaborative way to plan a long-term study.

- Imagine that you were planning a study of your school.

▶ Refer participants to *Building the Primary Classroom*

- On page 176 of *Building the Primary Classroom*, you will find guidelines for determining suitable topics for a study.

- As you look at these guidelines, ask yourself if a study of the school would be appropriate for primary grade children.

▶ Give instructions

- You will find piles of small pieces of paper at your tables. Think of as many words as you can that relate to the topic "school." Working individually, put one word on each piece of paper.

- Keep writing until you can't think of any other words.

▶ Notice when participants seem to have run out of ideas

- When you have finished, spread your words out on the table. Take a few minutes to read each other's words.

▶ When participants are ready, give the next instructions

- Working in your group, think about whether your words can be grouped together in categories.

- When you agree on some categories, group the words accordingly. Discard duplicate words.

Write "school" in the center of the chart

- Let's combine our ideas into a giant web. Let's hear one of your categories.

Write categories on a chart

- Does anybody have other categories?
  Some examples of categories might be:
  ◊ *equipment and machinery*
  ◊ *workers (jobs)*
  ◊ *physical characteristics*
  ◊ *food*
  ◊ *labels and signs*
  ◊ *activities*
  ◊ *materials*

Write words on chart under categories

- Let's take one category at a time and hear some words you listed in that category.

Refer participants to *Building the Primary Classroom*

- Look at the Harbor Chart on page 177 of the book. This is an example of how a web was generated for a different topic.

Summarize the session

- The purpose of this exercise was to focus on the range of possibilities in a topic.

- The process we used involved working together to generate multiple ideas.

- What are your thoughts about doing this as a group experience?

- Some people like to generate webs beginning with categories; others like to begin with words as we did today. We can revise and adjust the categories depending on the complexity or range of words suggested.

- It doesn't mean all the categories will be studied.

- It is an aid for thinking about resources and the interests of the children we teach, as well as particular curriculum objectives.

Chapter 4 Workshops

WORKSHOP TOPICS	PURPOSE	MATERIALS	APPROXIMATE TIME
Overview	To provide an overview of the content of chapter 4.	Notes, overhead, handout p. 106	5-10 minutes
Making Learning Meaningful	To show how an activity can engage children in meaningful learning.	Notes, chart paper, markers for each table p. 112	30-40 minutes
Helping Children Construct Knowledge (Relates to pp. 150-152)	To consider how teachers can create opportunities for children to actively construct knowledge.	Notes, handout, chart paper and markers p. 116	20-30 minutes
Stages in the Learning Process (Relates to pp. 155-158)	To identify ways teachers can enrich children's experiences at each stage in the learning process.	Notes, handout p. 120	20-30 minutes
Investigation, Representation, Reflection (Relates to pp. 166-171)	To consider how work times and long-term studies can be designed to guide children's learning.	Notes, handouts p. 124	30-45 minutes
A Learning Community	To explore how the first three strategies provide the foundation for guiding children's learning.	Notes, picture set p. 130	25-35 minutes
Generating Ideas for Long-Term Studies (Relates to pp. 172-181)	To demonstrate a process for thinking about study topics.	Notes, markers, small pieces of paper, chart paper p. 134	20-30 minutes
Planning a Long-Term Study	To generate initial plans for a study using a step-by-step process.	Notes, handouts, small pieces of paper p. 138	60-75 minutes

Planning a Long-Term Study

Note to teacher educators:

You may want tot assign the reading of pages 172-181 as preparation for this workshop session. If this is not feasible, begin the session by having everyone read those pages.

▶ Introduce the topic

- Today's session is an opportunity to use a step-by-step process to plan an actual study that would be appropriate for a group of children.

▶ Allow time for participants to form groups

- You will find it most helpful to work with others who share similar interests—either they work with the same age group or in the same school, or they plan to work with a particular grade.

▶ Distribute the Handout, "Topic Selection"

- The first step will be to identify appropriate topics—a topic that could be studied for several weeks or months and that contains a wide range of possible content and learning experiences.

- Begin by brainstorming on your own several possible topics for a long-term study.

- When you have five or more topics identified, use the guidelines on the handout to assess each one. Star any that you think meet all the guidlines.

▶ Allow sufficient time and provide assistance as needed

- Take some time to share the topics you starred with the other members of your group.

- Agree on one topic you want to focus on for today's session.

- If you need to re-arrange your groups to accommodate different interests, please do so.

▶ Distribute the Handout, "Brainstorming Content Ideas"

- This handout asks you to generate a web about your topic as we did when we made a web about our school or like the one on the Harbor on page 177 of *Building the Primary Classroom*.

▶ Give intructions

- Small pieces of paper are available for you to use to come up with all the words you can think of related to your topic.

▶ Assist groups with webbing

- Once you have your categories you can use the handout for your web.

▶ Distribute additional handouts. Assist groups as needed

- The remaining handouts are designed to walk you through the steps of planning a long-term study.

- I will pull us back together as a group at several points to share ideas.

- If you need assistance, I'm happy to be a resource for your group.

Topic Selection

Identify Possible Topics for a Long-Term Study:

_____

_____

_____

_____

Assess each topic using the following guidelines. Star those topics that meet the guidelines.

- The topic permits children to think, question, and solve problems as they investigate.

- The topic allows me to teach the required objectives of my school's curriculum.

- The skills and knowledge that children acquire from studying the topic can be applied to future living and learning.

- The topic is real, relevant to children's experiences, and is age-appropriate. The topic begins with phenomena that children can observe directly.

- Resources and materials related to the topic are readily available, (e.g., people to talk to, places to visit, books to read, and artifacts to examine).

- A wide variety of skills can be applied to the topic.

- The topic can be explored in various ways over an extended period of time.

Select one to focus on today: _____

Describe any additional reasons for choosing this topic.

_____

_____

_____

_____

Brainstorming Content Ideas

• Brainstorming ideas gives you <u>many</u> possibilities of directions the study could take.

• Brainstorming means getting <u>all</u> of your ideas down-even the ones that seem a bit crazy right now.

Make a list or a web of your ideas. See page 168 of *Building the Primary Classroom* for an example of a web.

Once you have your list or web, review it to consider resources you have or will need to locate.

Start a "Resource List" of books, people, pictures, artifacts, etc. as you brainstorm.

Use your "Brainstorm" list to think about the research you have to do to become more familiar with the topic.

Thinking About Curriculum Objectives

Think about how your topic might address curriculum objectives in each subject area. Brainstorm ideas. (See page 179 in *Building the Primary Classroom* for an example.) Focus on areas that are closely related to the topic.

_____ STUDY

SOCIAL STUDIES	SCIENTIFIC THINKING	MATHEMATICAL THINKING	LANGUAGE AND LITERACY	TECHNOLOGY AND THE ARTS

The Ways Children Construct Knowledge

What are some experiences you might plan to help children learn about the topic? Use the questions below to help you get started.

To identify opportunities for **investigation**, ask yourself these questions:

- How can the children conduct first-hand observations (trips, artifacts, experiments)?

- Who can the children interview (experts who can visit the classroom)?

- What books or other print materials are available that children can read independently?

- What songs, videos, computer software can be integrated with the study?

- What open-ended questions can be asked to encourage further thinking?

- How can families be involved in the study?

To identify opportunities for children to **represent** their learning, ask yourself these questions:

- What art projects lend themselves to this study (drawings, paintings, collages)?

- What kinds of models or construction projects can the children build as part of this study?

- What opportunities are there to make chart, graphs, or maps?

- What songs, skits, or plays might be related to the subject?

- What opportunities might there be to write interviews or record observations? What else can they write?

To identify opportunities for children to **reflect** on what they are learning, ask yourself:

- How can children keep a learning log or journal as a way to record what they are learning?

- How will I use meetings to encourage group reflection?

- What questions will I pose to encourage children to reflect on their learning?

- How can children return to their questions and assess whether or not they have found answers?

Action Plan

How will I introduce the study to children and invite families to participate?
(pages 180, steps 7 & 8)

How might the study be sequenced and how will I involve children in determining its sequence?
(page 181, step 9)

How will I conclude the study? (page 181, step 10)

5

Assessing
Children's
Learning

Chapter 5 Workshops

WORKSHOP TOPICS	PURPOSE	MATERIALS	APPROXIMATE TIME
Overview	To provide an overview of the content of chapter 5.	Notes, overhead, handout p. 150	5-10 minutes
Purposes of Assessment (Relates to pp. 190-203)	To consider assessment methods and the purposes they serve.	Notes, handout, chart paper and markers p. 156	30-40 minutes
Observation (Relates to pp. 204-207)	To explore the difference between recording facts and judgments.	Notes, chart paper, markers (Videotape, if necessary) p. 160	15-20 minutes
Techniques for Recording Observations [Relates to pp. 208-209]	To consider a variety of techniques for recording observations. To emphasize the importance of planning and routines in making observations.	Notes, chart paper and markers p. 164	15-20 minutes
Collecting, Reviewing, and Evaluating Children's Work [Relates to pp. 209-213]	To consider what can be learned from studying children's work. To evaluate the types of work that should be collected.	Notes, work samples from teachers' classrooms p. 166	45-60 minutes

Overview

▶ Introduce the strategy

- Assessment is the process of gathering information about children to answer questions and make decisions about their education.

- Assessment is the fifth strategy for in *Building the Primary Classroom*. When teachers have a method for collecting information on children's development and learning, they can adapt curriculum and plan instruction so that every child experiences success.

▶ Put on overhead

- This overhead highlights three issues in our discussion of assessment: 1) understanding what assessment is and its various purposes; 2) describing the type of assessment that is appropriate for planning curriculum; and 3) highlighting some specific approaches for assessing children's progress.

- I will give a brief overview of what is addressed in each section. You have this as a handout if you wish to take notes.

▶ Discuss understanding assessment

- Assessment includes the tools and processes used to answer questions. Part of assessment involves gathering data or documentation; another part involves evaluation or a comparison to a standard.

- Currently, there is much debate about assessment. To determine the type of assessment that is most appropriate, we must first know its purpose and how the results will be used.

- Many people today are concerned about the value of administering certain kinds of standardized tests to young children. There are issues related to fairness as well as the fact that testing sometimes narrows the curriculum because teachers tend to spend time preparing children for the test.

- Appropriate assessment relies on an approach that outlines reasonable and age-appropriate expectations for children. To assess children accurately and fairly, procedures should be aligned with the curriculum, ongoing, in context, and comprehensive.

Discuss how assessment supports instruction

- When assessment is tied closely to curriculum, the information teachers collect can offer an in-depth portrait of what children are learning and how they are progressing.

- Assessment should be a critical first step in planning curriculum. If the assessment approach is compatible with the goals and objectives of the curriculum, then assessment information helps you know what to teach, when children are ready to learn particular skills and concepts, and how to structure learning experiences.

- Ongoing assessment in the classroom helps teachers to individualize the curriculum. Teachers can plan instruction that is responsive to children's needs and builds on their strengths.

- Observation in a variety of classroom situations is a valuable assessment tool.

- An approach to assessment that involves children by giving them criteria to evaluate their work and helping them set personal goals increases their investment in their work. Classroom rubrics are useful tools to make goals and expectations explicit and enhance objectivity and fairness in assessment.

- A comprehensive approach to assessment that is tied to the curriculum enables teachers to share children's progress in a meaningful way. Family members will have a much better picture of children's progress when they can see concrete evidence of children's work over time.

Discuss how teachers assess children's learning

- When teachers have a framework for assessing children's work, they can ensure that observations are focused and that all areas of a child's development and learning are assessed.

- *Building the Primary Classroom* describes three components of a framework for assessment.

- First, teachers need to systematically observe children and document what they see in the context of classroom activities.

- A second component of a comprehensive approach to assessment includes collecting, reviewing, and evaluating children's work over time.

- The third component is a method to report assessment information to families in an understandable and comprehensive way.

- When teachers have conducted ongoing observations and collected samples of children's work over time, they have extensive assessment information to share with families or others who need to know about children's growth and progress.

▶ Summarize the Overview

- Appropriate assessment of children's learning is vital to making informed decisions about their education.

Assessing Children's Learning

- Understanding Assessment

- How Assessment Supports Instruction

- How Teachers Assess Children's Learning

Chapter 5 Workshops

WORKSHOP TOPICS	PURPOSE	MATERIALS	APPROXIMATE TIME
Overview	To provide an overview of the content of chapter 5.	Notes, overhead, handout p. 150	5-10 minutes
Purposes of Assessment (Relates to pp. 190-203)	To consider assessment methods and the purposes they serve.	Notes, handout, chart paper and markers p. 156	30-40 minutes
Observation (Relates to pp. 204-207)	To explore the difference between recording facts and judgments.	Notes, chart paper, markers (Videotape, if necessary) p. 160	15-20 minutes
Techniques for Recording Observations (Relates to pp. 208-209)	To consider a variety of techniques for recording observations. To emphasize the importance of planning and routines in making observations.	Notes, chart paper and markers p. 164	15-20 minutes
Collecting, Reviewing, and Evaluating Children's Work (Relates to pp. 209-213)	To consider what can be learned from studying children's work. To evaluate the types of work that should be collected.	Notes, work samples from teachers' classrooms p. 166	45-60 minutes

Purposes of Assessment

▶ **Introduce the activity**

- This activity is designed to help you think about all the various purposes of assessment and the methods or strategies you might use to assess children.

▶ **Distribute handout, "Purposes of Assessment"**

- Working at your table, please discuss with your group and respond to question #1.

- When you have completed question 1, take a few minutes on your own to respond to questions 2 and 3.

▶ **When participants are ready, invite them to share their ideas**

- Would anyone like to share their responses to these questions?

▶ **Give instructions for jigsaw reading**

- Pages 190-203 of *Building the Primary Classroom* discuss "Understanding Assessment" and "How Assessment Supports Instruction." Please divide into two groups at your table and have each group choose a section to read. After you read, discuss the two sections with each other.

▶ **Ask participants to compare their reading with what they wrote**

- Compare your thoughts about the reading with what you wrote earlier on the handout.

▶ **When participants are ready, invite people to share their ideas**

- What questions, reactions, or new ideas do you have as a result of today's session?

Purposes of Assessment

Working with your group:

1. Generate a list of the various purposes of assessment.

2. What methods or strategies are you currently using to assess children? Which of the above purposes do they serve?

3. Are there any purposes of assessment for which you lack effective strategies? What might you try?

Chapter 5 Workshops

WORKSHOP TOPICS	PURPOSE	MATERIALS	APPROXIMATE TIME
Overview	To provide an overview of the content of chapter 5.	Notes, overhead, handout p. 150	5-10 minutes
Purposes of Assessment (Relates to pp. 190-203)	To consider assessment methods and the purposes they serve.	Notes, handout, chart paper and markers p. 156	30-40 minutes
Observation (Relates to pp. 204-207)	To explore the difference between recording facts and judgments	Notes, chart paper, markers (Videotape, if necessary) p. 160	15-20 minutes
Techniques for Recording Observations (Relates to pp. 208-209)	To consider a variety of techniques for recording observations. To emphasize the importance of planning and routines in making observations.	Notes, chart paper and markers p. 164	15-20 minutes
Collecting, Reviewing, and Evaluating Children's Work (Relates to pp. 209-213)	To consider what can be learned from studying children's work. To evaluate the types of work that should be collected.	Notes, work samples from teachers' classrooms p. 166	45-60 minutes

Observation

Note to teacher educators:

Decide in advance whether you will show a videotape of children or whether you will role play the part of a child in a classroom. If you do a role play, try to create a scene with some ambiguity in your actions. (E.g. Are you really paying attention to your reading even though you are looking around?) For example, you might pick up a book, hold it upside down for a moment, then position it correctly. Read for a few seconds, look up, read, get up but continue to read, trip over something, drop the book, pick it up, look at the back of the book, look at the back cover, sit down, read, stare at the ceiling, put the book on the floor.

▶ Introduce the topic

- Observation is part of everyday life in the classroom. During work times when children are engaged in investigation and representation activities, teachers can watch what children do, listen to what they say, and talk with them about the products they create.

- It's not necessary or possible to observe and record everything that children say and do.

- Organizing a plan for what and how to observe and record, and then spending a few minutes a day doing so, yields a wealth of valuable information.

▶ Introduce the activity

- We are going to practice observing and recording. Please take out a blank sheet of paper.

- Imagine that I am a ___ year-old child. Pretend it is independent reading time (if you follow the role play example suggested above). You are the teacher observing me (or show a videotape).

▶ Do the roleplay or show the videotape

- Record what you observe. I will begin now.

▶ **Ask participants what they wrote and record on chart paper**

- Let's go around and hear what people wrote. I'll record it on the chart.

▶ **Read the list and ask which are judgments and which are facts**

- Now, we'll read over our list of observations. Let's think about which phrases are factual and which reflect a judgment or interpretation. I'll put a line through the ones that are judgments.

▶ **Summarize the session**

- One of the hardest aspects of observing children is documenting their actions and words, rather than our impressions of them. It is normal for our interests, culture, beliefs, and experiences to influence our observations.

- When we observe for the purpose of assessing children, we need to make every effort to guard against our biases by focusing on actions and avoiding judgments about behavior.

- When only the child's actions are recorded and judgments are omitted, it is possible to consider a variety of explanations for behaviors and to be open to different ways of interpreting a child's motives.

- Therefore, in recording and observing, try to write down only what you see and hear. Questions and concerns can be documented separately.

- Collecting observations made at various times of the day, over time, and in many situations gives us a great deal of data for reflection.

- Factual observation records help you to make instructional plans for children and give you information needed to report to families and to complete school reports.

- Documenting observations enables teachers to detect patterns in a child's behavior, or the source of a problem. Then, teachers can devise a plan and monitor the plan's effectiveness.

▶ **Give follow-up activity assignment. Refer to *Building the Primary Classroom***

- Before our next session, please do a two-minute observation of a child and bring it with you.

- Review the two examples on page 207 and reflect on the difference between an objective record and one containing judgments and interpretation.

Chapter 5 Workshops

WORKSHOP TOPICS	PURPOSE	MATERIALS	APPROXIMATE TIME
Overview	To provide an overview of the content of chapter 5.	Notes, overhead, handout p. 150	5-10 minutes
Purposes of Assessment (Relates to pp. 190-203)	To consider assessment methods and the purposes they serve.	Notes, handout, chart paper and markers p. 156	30-40 minutes
Observation (Relates to pp. 204-207)	To explore the difference between recording facts and judgments.	Notes, chart paper, markers (Videotape, if necessary) p. 160	15-20 minutes
Techniques for Recording Observations (Relates to pp. 208-209)	To consider a techniques for recording observations. To To emphasize the importance of planning and routines in making observations	Notes, chart paper and markers p. 164	15-20 minutes
Collecting, Reviewing, and Evaluating Children's Work (Relates to pp. 209-213)	To consider what can be learned from studying children's work. To evaluate the types of work that should be collected.	Notes, work samples from teachers' classrooms p. 166	45-60 minutes

Techniques for Recording Observations

Note to teacher educators:
This workshop activity assumes that participants have had some experience in a classroom. The follow-up assignment is an observation of a child.

▶ **Introduce the topic**

- Teachers observe children all the time, but it's difficult to remember to write things down and keep records.

- Today we are going to consider techniques for recording observations and then discuss our own personal strategies.

▶ **Introduce the reading**

- Please begin by reading pages 208-209 of *Building the Primary Classroom* on techniques for recording observations.

▶ **When participants are done, ask them to share their ideas at their table**

- Let's share techniques you may have tried and brainstorm ideas about what might work for you.

▶ **Reconvene the group and write ideas on chart paper**

- Would each group please give us a summary?

▶ **Summarize the session and give follow-up assignment**

- Because planning time to do observations and creating a routine are so essential, I'd like to ask each of you to write down one time during the week when you will plan to observe children.

- At our next session, you can report on how it worked.

Chapter 5 Workshops

WORKSHOP TOPICS	PURPOSE	MATERIALS	APPROXIMATE TIME
Overview	To provide an overview of the content of chapter 5.	Notes, overhead, handout p. 150	5-10 minutes
Purposes of Assessment (Relates to pp. 190-203)	To consider assessment methods and the purposes they serve.	Notes, handout, chart paper and markers p. 156	30-40 minutes
Observation (Relates to pp. 204-207)	To explore the difference between recording facts and judgments.	Notes, chart paper, markers (Videotape, if necessary) p. 160	15-20 minutes
Techniques for Recording Observations (Relates to pp. 208-209)	To consider a variety of techniques for recording observations. To emphasize the importance of planning and routines in making observations.	Notes, chart paper and markers p. 164	15-20 minutes
Collecting, Reviewing, and Evaluating Children's Work (Relates to p. 209-213)	To consider what can be learned from studying children's work. To evaluate the types of work that should be collected.	Notes, work samples from teachers' classrooms p. 166	45-60 minutes

Collecting, Reviewing, and Evaluating Children's Work

Note to teacher educators:
Ask participants to bring some samples of children's work with them to the workshop.

▶ **Introduce the topic**

- The work children create each day in the classroom provides concrete evidence of what they are learning. Collecting, reviewing, and evaluating children's work on a regular basis is important.

- Children are more motivated when they receive specific feedback about their work.

- Studying the products children create helps you learn about how children think, what they can do, and what they are ready to learn next.

- Samples of children's work can be organized into a portfolio to create a portrait of the child's growth and progress.

▶ **Introduce the activity and participate in the discussions at each table**

- Share with the people at your table the samples you have brought with you.

- Consider two questions as you look at each piece of work:
    ◊ What can this child do?
    ◊ What is this child ready to learn next?

▶ **Introduce the reading**

- In *Building the Primary Classroom,* pages 210-211, you will find a discussion of "Studying Children's Work."

- Take a few minutes to read these pages.

- Does it give you additional thoughts about the samples you brought today?

Encourage further discussion at tables

- Talk with the people at your table about what ideas you want to use.

Reconvene the whole group

- Ask the groups to report on their key findings.

Introduce the concept of portfolios

- The word portfolios is used a great deal today as people begin to think about more appropriate ways of assessing young children.

- As described in *Building the Primary Classroom*, portfolios are purposeful collections of a child's work.

- It is not simply a scrapbook or folder of children's work; it is a tool that is organized in such a way that the teacher, the child, and the child's family can learn about the quality of the child's work and observe progress over time.

Follow-up assignment

- Portfolios can be a valuable assessment tool when they are organized according to a plan.

- Please read the section on portfolios in *Building the Primary Classroom*, pages 211-213.

6

BUILDING A PARTNERSHIP WITH FAMILIES

Chapter 6 Workshops

WORKSHOP TOPICS	PURPOSE	MATERIALS	APPROXIMATE TIME
Overview	To provide an overview of the content of chapter 6.	Notes, overhead, handout p. 172	5-10 minutes
Different Perspectives (Relates to pp. 220-221)	To develop awareness of how parents and teachers may view one another and identify strategies for developing an effective partnership.	Notes, chart paper and markers p. 178	20-30 minutes
Self-Awareness (Relates to pp.221-225)	To consider the influence of one's own cultural orientation and its impact on forming partnerships with families.	Notes, handout p. 182	30-40 minutes
Approaches to Involving Families [Relates to pp. 226-236]	To identify multiple ways families can be involved in the life of the classroom.	Notes p. 186	30-40 minutes
How Involving Families Supports the Other Strategies [Relates to pp. 237-248]	To show how involving families supports teachers' implementation of the first five strategies.	Notes, handout p. 188	30-40 minutes

Overview

▶ **Introduce the strategy**

- Teachers and parents share the same goals: to help children become successful learners.

- The family is the child's first educational environment.

- Children benefit most when they see their teachers and families sharing common goals and working together in ways that are respectful.

- The sixth strategy for building the primary classroom addresses the importance of building partnership with children's families.

▶ **Put on overhead**

- It is essential for someone of importance in the child's home life to develop a positive relationship with the child's teacher and be supported by the school community.

- I'll use this overhead to provide an overview of what is addressed in this chapter. You have this as a handout if you wish to take notes.

▶ **Discuss setting the stage**

- Trust is the foundation of positive relationships. Prior experiences of both parents and teachers may influence their perspectives of one another and interfere with the building of trust.

- As educators, it is in our interest to assume that all parents want their children to succeed. This enables us to enter relationships with families with an open mind.

- Not all parents can participate in the same way. For some, getting their children to school each day is a significant accomplishment and demonstrates a commitment to their child's education.

- Teachers who focus on collaboration and outreach and do not measure success on parents' attendance at school activities are more likely to be successful building partnerships.

- When the cultural background of the teacher and family are different, the teacher is responsible for bridging the gap. This begins by learning as much as possible about the child's home culture and avoiding forming judgments prematurely.

Discuss eight approaches

- This section of *Building the Primary Classroom* highlights specific ideas teachers can try.

- Building relationships with families asks a great deal of teachers. It takes time and effort.

- When teachers are successful, their jobs can be easier and more rewarding.

- When the school as a whole is supportive of family partnerships, more is accomplished.

Discuss how involving families supports the first five strategies

- A partnership with families supports the first five strategies of *Building the Primary Classroom* as well.

- Parents can help you know the children; they can both contribute to the classroom community and help children make connections between their home and school communities.

- Families are better able to support your classroom structure if they know what it is all about.

- When families understand what you are teaching, they can support children's learning.

- Collaborating with families about assessment can increase understanding and further support children's needs.

Discuss families in need of special services

- Teachers cannot possibly meet the needs of all the children they reach.

- Families in need of special services should be referred to school counselors and community agencies.

- In communities where school-home collaboration have been the most successful, a group of teachers or the principal has taken the initiative to create partnerships with organizations that can meet parents' need for medical, dental, counseling, employment, and other services.

Building a Partnership With Families

- Setting the Stage for a Positive Relationship

- Eight Approaches to Involving Families

- How Involving Families Supports the First Five Strategies

- Families in Need of Special Services

Chapter 6 Workshops

WORKSHOP TOPICS	PURPOSE	MATERIALS	APPROXIMATE TIME
Overview	To provide an overview of the content of chapter 6.	Notes, overhead, handout p. 172	5-10 minutes
Different Perspectives (Relates to pp. 220-221)	To develop awareness of how parents and teachers may view one another and identify strategies for developing an effective partnership.	Notes, chart paper and markers p. 178	20-30 minutes
Self-Awareness (Relates to pp.221-225)	To consider the influence of one's own cultural orientation and its impact on forming partnerships with families.	Notes, handout p. 182	30-40 minutes
Approaches to Involving Families (Relates to pp. 226-236)	To identify multiple ways families can be involved in the life of the classroom.	Notes p. 186	30-40 minutes
How Involving Families Supports the Other Strategies (Relates to pp. 237-248)	To show how involving families supports teachers' implementation of the first five strategies.	Notes, handout p. 188	30-40 minutes

Different Perspectives

▶ **Introduce the topic**

- Our past experiences influence how we view people and events.

- If parents feel they have not been treated well by teachers or administrators in the past, they have no reason to trust their child's current teachers.

- If teachers have had experiences with parents who were not supportive of their efforts, they may view all parents as "problems."

▶ **Explain the activity**

- We are going to do an activity which requires you, figuratively, "to get in each other's shoes."

- I'd like each table to count off beginning with #1.

▶ **Allow the groups to work for about 10 minutes**

- The odd numbered tables are teachers. Your task is to brainstorm how parents view you. What are the ideas and assumptions parents have of teachers?

- The even numbered tables are parents. Your task is to think about how teachers view you. What are the ideas and assumptions teachers have of parents?

- Choose a recorder at your table to document ideas.

▶ **Prepare 2 charts: 1) How Parents View Teachers 2) How Teachers View Parents**

- Let's take some ideas from each table beginning with the teachers and I'll record them on these charts.

- As you look over these assumptions, do you have any thoughts about their impact on forming a partnership with families?

▶ **Give instructions**

- At your tables, talk about strategies that might be effective for overcoming any negative assumptions.

▶ **Reconvene the group**

- Let's hear some of your ideas.

Chapter 6 Workshops

WORKSHOP TOPICS	PURPOSE	MATERIALS	APPROXIMATE TIME
Overview	To provide an overview of the content of chapter 6.	Notes, overhead, handout p. 172	5-10 minutes
Different Perspectives (Relates to	To develop awareness of how parents and teachers may view one another and identify strategies for developing an effective partnership.	Notes, chart paper and markers p. 178	20-30 minutes pp. 220-221)
Self-Awareness (Relates to pp. 221-225)	To consider the influence of one's own cultural orientation and its impact on forming partnerships with families.	Notes, handout p. 182	30-40 minutes
Approaches to Involving Families pp. 226-236)	To identify multiple ways families can be involved in the life of the classroom.	Notes p. 186	30-40 minutes (Relates to
How Involving Families Supports the Other Strategies (Relates to pp. 237-248)	To show how involving families supports teachers' implementation of the first five strategies.	Notes, handout p. 188	30-40 minutes

Self-Awareness

▶ **Introduce the topic**

- Awareness of one's own culture helps us to better understand and connect with people from other cultures.

- Understanding and respecting differences is essential in building a partnership with families.

▶ **Distribute Handout, "Understanding Culture"**

- The questions on this handout are taken from *Building the Primary Classroom* (pages 223-224).

- Read each one, then write down any ideas that come to mind.

- You don't have to share your responses with anyone unless you wish to do so.

▶ **Allow 10-20 minutes**

- When you have finished writing, take a few minutes to reflect on your responses.

- Consider the impact these assumptions, attitudes, and expectations may have on your ability to build a partnership with children's families.

- Now find a partner and share any insights you may have from this exercise.

▶ **Summarize the session**

- Would any partners like to share their reactions/thoughts with the group?

- Some of us are more aware of our cultural influences than others, but each of us has a cultural lens through which we view experiences and other people.

- When we are more aware of our own biases and expectations, we can then begin to learn about the specific cultures of the children we teach.

Understanding Culture

What were the messages you received about you own culture and people from other cultures when you were growing up? Write down any ideas that come to mind as you read the following questions.

1) How was your racial/ethnic identity described to you? Were there any characteristics of your group that were described as special?

2) What were the early messages that you received about other ethnic/racial groups?

3) How has the media's labels of different groups influenced you at different times during your life?

4) What messages did you receive about your family's socio-economic position?

5) What types of exposure did you have to people with mental or physical disabilities? What were you told about these people? How did you feel when you were around them?

6) What messages did you receive about "being smart"? Were certain groups of people smarter than others?

7) How important was the ability to express yourself verbally? Was it acceptable to interject your opinion when others were speaking?

8) Was it okay to be noisy and physically active in your home/community?

9) Were you exposed to families that did not have a traditional family structure (husband/wife)? What were you told about non-traditional family structures?

Chapter 6 Workshops

WORKSHOP TOPICS	PURPOSE	MATERIALS	APPROXIMATE TIME
Overview	To provide an overview of the content of chapter 6.	Notes, overhead, handout p. 172	5-10 minutes
Different Perspectives (Relates to pp. 220-221)	To develop awareness of how parents and teachers may view one another and identify strategies for developing an effective partnership.	Notes, chart paper and markers p. 178	20-30 minutes
Self-Awareness (Relates to pp.221-225)	To consider the influence of one's own cultural orientation and its impact on forming partnerships with families.	Notes, handout p. 182	30-40 minutes
Approaches to Involving Families (Relates to pp. 226-236)	To identify multiple ways families can be involved in the life of the classroom.	Notes p. 186	30-40 minutes
How Involving Families Supports the Other (Relates to pp. 237-248)	To show how involving families supports teachers' implementation of the first five strategies.	Notes, handout p. 188	30-40 minutes Strategies

Approaches to Involving Families

Note to teacher educators:
Write the eight approaches to involving families on a chart before beginning the workshop (see page 218).

▶ **Introduce the activity**

- There are many ways to involve families.

- The chart lists eight approaches described in *Building the Primary Classroom.*

- You probably have many ideas for involving families that fall under each of these approaches.

▶ **Give instructions and note when participants seem to have run out of ideas**

- Work with the people at your table to share what you already do or could do in each of these categories.

▶ **Introduce jigsaw reading**

- On pages 226-236 in *Building the Primary Classroom* these eight approaches are discussed.

- Divide up the eight sections so that each person at your table is reading one or two, depending on the number people in your group.

- After reading selections in the book, share with the other members of your group ideas you want to try, as well as your reactions.

▶ **Conclude the session**

- Hopefully you have some additional ideas for ways to extend what you currently do. You can think about what you may want to add. Or perhaps you will now think about what you might do when you have your own classroom of students.

Chapter 6 Workshops

WORKSHOP TOPICS	PURPOSE	MATERIALS	APPROXIMATE TIME
Overview	To provide an overview of the content of chapter 6.	Notes, overhead, handout p. 172	5-10 minutes
Different Perspectives (Relates to pp. 220-221)	To develop awareness of how parents and teachers may view one another and identify strategies for developing an effective partnership.	Notes, chart paper and markers p. 178	20-30 minutes
Self-Awareness (Relates to pp.221-225)	To consider the influence of one's own cultural orientation and its impact on forming partnerships with families.	Notes, handout p. 182	30-40 minutes
Approaches to Involving Families (Relates to pp. 226-236)	To identify multiple ways families can be involved in the life of the classroom.	Notes p. 186	30-40 minutes
How Involving Families Supports the Other Strategies (Relates to pp. 237-248)	To show how involving families implementation supports teachers' of the first five strategies.	Notes, handout p. 188	30-40 minutes

How Involving Families Supports the Other Strategies

▶ Introduce the topic

- Developing a partnership with families makes a teacher's job easier.

- Rather than looking at parent involvement as one more task, it's helpful to examine how a partnership supports the first five strategies for *Building the Primary Classroom*.

▶ Distribute Handout, "Building a Partnership with Families"

- This handout provides a space for you to record your ideas on how a partnership with families helps you to know the children you teach, build a classroom community, establish a clear structure, guide children's learning, and assess children learning.

- Each group should select one strategy so that each of the five are covered. Let me know when you've decided.

- Reflect on what you know about the strategy you picked.

- Brainstorm together how a partnership with families could help you to implement that strategy.

- Take about 15 minutes to brainstorm together.

▶ After 15 minutes (or more if needed), give the next instruction

- Now take a few minutes to read through the suggestions on your strategy in *Building the Primary Classroom*.

- You will find where your strategy begins by looking at the table of contents for Chapter 6 on page 218.

- Discuss any ideas you want to add to your section of the chart.

- I'll ask someone from each group to give a brief report on your discussion in about 10 minutes.

▶ **Allow 10-15 minutes before reconvening the group for reports**

- Let's hear a brief report from each group.

- Do you have any questions, reactions, or new ideas as a result of today's session?

Building a Partnership With Families

Families and educators share the same goals: to help children become successful learners and develop social competence. Teachers who take time to build a partnership with each child's family gain critically important allies in creating exciting classrooms and confident students. It supports each of the first five strategies for *Building the Primary Classroom*.

Strategy	How a Partnership with Families Enhances This Strategy
Knowing the Children	
Building a Classroom Community	
Establishing a Clear Structure	
Guiding Children's Learning	
Assessing Children's Learning	